# Mike the Tiger

# The Roar of LSU

*Second Edition*

# DAVID G. BAKER *and* W. SHELDON BIVIN

Louisiana State University Press | Baton Rouge

Published by Louisiana State University Press
Copyright © 2003, 2013 by Louisiana State University Press
All rights reserved
Manufactured in South Korea
First printing

Designer: Laura Roubique Gleason
Typefaces: Thirsty Rough, display; Minion Pro, text
Printer and binder: Pacom

Mike VI sleeping (dedication page): Christine Russell
Mike VI stalking (opposite Contents): Christine Russell
Mike VI with his ball (page ix): Tim Morgan
Photographs by C. C. Lockwood are copyrighted C. C.
    Lockwood 2003.

Library of Congress Cataloging-in-Publication Data
Baker, David G., 1956–
  Mike the tiger : the roar of LSU / David G. Baker and W.
Sheldon Bivin.
      pages   cm.
  ISBN 978-0-8071-5322-2 (cloth : alk. paper)  1. Louisiana
State University (Baton Rouge, La.)—Mascots—History.
2. LSU Tigers (Football team)—History.  3. Mike (Tiger)
I. Bivin, W. Sheldon.  II. Title.
  GV858.L65B34 2013
  796.332′63076318—dc23
                         2013010272

*This book is dedicated to all who love LSU and Mike the Tiger.*

# Contents

# Mike the Tiger

A Louisiana Tiger

*Courtesy National Archives*

# THE LSU TIGERS, 1861–1936

Just how did the LSU student athletes become known as the Tigers? To answer this question we have to go back to a dark period in the history of this great nation. North and South were about to engage in the bloodiest war ever fought on the North American continent. On January 26, 1861, Louisiana seceded from the Union. Civil War appeared imminent. In communities all over Louisiana, companies of soldiers were organized to serve in the Confederate army. One of the first companies formed gave itself the name Tiger Rifles. The Tiger Rifles were under the leadership of Captain Alex White, a veteran of the Mexican War. To say that the Tigers were colorful is not only literally true but an understatement of comical proportions. The company had been outfitted with outlandish uniforms similar to those worn by French Zouaves. They wore scarlet skull caps, red shirts, open blue jackets, and baggy blue and white striped pants tucked

These miniature replicas show the colorful uniform worn by the Louisiana Tigers.

Major Chatham Roberdeau Wheat, C.S.A., commander of the 1st Louisiana Special Battalion, which included the Tiger Rifles.

*Courtesy Mrs. William Elam*

had served time in a penitentiary for pistol-whipping a passenger on a steamboat. The Tigers were commonly referred to derisively as "wharf rats" and a variety of other unsavory names.

Soon another company, the Old Dominion Guards, was recruited by the charismatic and soldierly Major Chatham Roberdeau Wheat, one of the most colorful figures of the day. The thirty-five-year-old Wheat was a native of Virginia but had spent a considerable portion of his life in Louisiana, mostly in New Orleans. Wheat was a lawyer by profession, though he seems to have spent more time as a soldier of fortune than as a practicing attorney. He had fought as a mercenary in Cuba, Mexico, Nicaragua, and Italy. When war broke out at Fort Sumter on April 12, Wheat was one of the most experienced soldiers in either army. At six foot four and 275 pounds and with the social graces of an aristocrat and the fighting spirit of a wild animal, he was a natural leader. Soon a third company, the Walker Guards, was formed. By now, Major Wheat had his mind set on forming a battalion, so he turned command of the Old Dominion Guards over to Captain Obed P. Miller. Later, two more companies were placed under Wheat's command: the Delta Rangers and the Rough and Ready Rangers. The Rough and Readies would later be disbanded and replaced in Wheat's battalion with the Catahoula Guerrillas. In

into white leggings. On their hats they painted pictures or mottoes such as "Lincoln's Life or a Tiger's Death," and "Tiger by Nature." In addition to the gaudy colors of their uniforms, the men themselves were anything but dull. Mostly young Irishmen, many of them were criminals. In fact, even Captain White

June 1861 the 1st Special Battalion was officially commissioned, with Major Wheat as commanding officer. Over the course of the war, a total of 416 men would serve under the battalion's colors. Eventually, Wheat's battalion was permanently assigned to Brigadier General Richard "Dick" Taylor's Louisiana Brigade, along with the 6th, 7th, 8th, and 9th Regiments of Louisiana Volunteers. Major Wheat was finally killed in battle at Gaines's Mill on June 27, 1862. The battalion had been so decimated that it was disbanded in August 1862, and the remaining men were reassigned to regiments serving in Virginia.

While the "tiger" label originally applied only to Wheat's Company B, the Tiger Rifles, the characterization fit the whole battalion. The majority of the men were drinkers, brawlers, thieves, or ex-convicts and were considered the dregs of New Orleans. It wasn't long before all members of Wheat's battalion were called "Tigers." Later, the name "Louisiana Tigers" was applied to all Louisiana infantry, but by that time it was not so much because of their unruly behavior but because of their tremendous courage and ferocity in battle. Louisiana infantry were part of General Robert E. Lee's Army of Northern Virginia and proved to be among the most valuable soldiers. Lee's Tigers, as they came to be known, did their duty and performed with great heroism. They fought from First Manassas to the very last

Confederate charge of the war, which they led, near Appomattox Courthouse on April 9, 1865. One gruesome testimony to their courage and fighting spirit was their death rate. By the end of the war it had reached 23 percent. To grasp the enormity of such sacrifice, one must realize that in all wars the number of wounded survivors greatly exceeds the number of dead. Additional testimony to the fighting spirit of the Tigers is revealed in the following farewell address from General Clement Anselm Evans to Colonel Eugene Waggaman's brigade on April 11, 1865:

> The sad hour has arrived when we who served in the Confederate Army so long together must part, at least for a time. . . . But to you, Colonel, and to our brother officers and brother soldiers . . . I claim to say that you can carry with you the proud conscience that in the estimation of your commanders you have done your duty. Tell Louisiana, when you reach her shores, that her sons in the Army of Northern Virginia have made her illustrious upon every battle ground, from first Manassas to the last desperate blow struck by your command on the hills of Appomattox, and tell her, too, that as in the first, so in the last, the enemy fled before the valor of your charging lines. . . . For you, and for your gallant officers and devoted men, I shall always cherish the most pleasing memories, and when I say farewell, it is with a full heart, which beats an earnest prayer to Almighty God for your future happiness.

Major David F. Boyd of the 9th Louisiana Volunteers may have been the first to propose the Tiger nickname the football team would adopt.

shared his premonition of his own impending death. It was Major Boyd who made sure that the last request of his friend and fellow soldier was fulfilled, that he was buried where he fell. Through battle after battle, Major Boyd developed tremendous respect for Wheat's Tigers and for their fearless, and now fallen, commander. The memory of those ferocious Fighting Tigers would stay with Major Boyd long after the din and destruction of war had passed. And in a more peaceful time, the memory of those Tigers and their master would be honored at one of the great universities of the South.

Organized in 1893 by Dr. Charles E. Coates, LSU football also has a colorful history. Dr. Coates obtained membership for LSU in the large Southern Intercollegiate Athletic Association (SIAA), of which LSU was a member until 1923. Dr. Coates, a chemistry professor from Baltimore, served as the head football coach during the team's maiden year. Dr. Coates was so dedicated to establishing football as a sport at LSU that he personally drove nails into shoes to fashion cleats for the team. The team was led by captain and quarterback Ruffin G. Pleasant, who would later serve as state attorney general from 1912 to 1916 and then as governor of Louisiana from 1916 to 1920. The "season" of 1893 consisted of one game, against Tulane University on November 25, which Tulane won 34–0.

One of the soldiers in the 9th Louisiana Volunteers was Major David F. Boyd. His regiment served in Taylor's Louisiana Brigade along with Wheat's 1st Special Battalion, during the Valley campaign of Brigadier General Thomas J. "Stonewall" Jackson. The two junior officers became great friends. Major Boyd was one of the first with whom Wheat

The 1896 football team that earned the nickname "Tigers." Pictured are, from left: back row (*standing*), A. E. Chevanne, Wiltz Ledbetter, Justin Daspit, Sidney Snyder, Jim Harp, Lt. Gallop, P. D. Staples, A. T. Barbin, J. T. Westbrook; center row (*seated*), Hughes Arrighi, Ned Scott, Phil Huych, W. S. Slaughter; front row, George Schoenberger, Sam Gourrier, Sam Atkinson, Gordon Nicholson, A. P. Daspit.

*Garland McManus*

Though off to a slow start, the football program gathered steam rapidly, posting a 2-1-0 record in the 1894 season under head coach Albert P. Simmons, with victories over Natchez (26–0) and Centenary (30–0). The only loss (6–26), and the year's only SIAA game, was against Ole Miss. That year the team captain was a fullback by the colorful name of Samuel Marmaduke Dinwidie Clark. In 1895, still under Coach Simmons, the team had its first undefeated season, going 3-0-0 under the leadership of captain and quarterback J. E. Snyder. As significant as the accomplishments of the 1895 season were, the team achieved national attention in 1896, with a perfect 6-0-0 record and cochampionship of the SIAA under Coach Allen W. Jeardeau.

The pride and excitement generated by such

ATHLETICS

LSU

Tiger illustration from the 1911 *Gumbo* yearbook.

Louisiana Tigers came flooding back to professor and former LSU president David F. Boyd and that it is quite likely that it was Boyd who suggested the tiger as the symbol of the university and its football team. While the name was modified slightly in 1955 to "the Fighting Tigers," most still simply refer to the team as "the Tigers."

Naming the team the Tigers seems to have been a logical choice for several reasons. First, the great military tradition of Louisiana's soldiers not only of the Civil War but of all the wars in which they have served is honored and commemorated in the name. Secondly, nothing represents a university like its mascot. The mascot should present a positive and stirring image of the school. Knowing this, many collegiate teams of the past, and even of the present, have borne names of ferocious animals. What more ferocious animal is there than a tiger? To this day, LSU Tiger fans are proud to compare their regal tiger mascot with the dogs, cats, camels, antelopes, sheep, horses, cattle, fish, dolphins, seals, reptiles, amphibians, birds, badgers, armadillos, rodents, kangaroos, apes, bears, pigs, insects, and even banana slug mascots of other college teams. And finally, history has proved the Tiger mascot to be appropriate in yet another way. Like other cats, tigers are most active at night, and one of the many legends surrounding Tiger football

accomplishments prompted the student body to seek a "nickname" for the team. Time has hidden the story of who first proposed naming the team the Tigers. Some sources credit Coach Coates with the idea. Others suggest that memories of Major Wheat and the

is that the team plays better at night. From 1960 to 1990, the team recorded a nighttime winning percentage in Tiger Stadium of 78.5 percent. During the same years, the team won only 39.5 percent of games played during the day. Although the tiger theme caught on instantly, for almost forty years other mascots continued to be suggested. Nicknames brought up for consideration included the Babies, the Roosters, the Alligators, and the Pirates. But with each passing year the tiger theme became more accepted.

From 1896 to 1924, Tiger fans would carry papier-mâché tigers to the football games. Most of these were destroyed by opposing fans almost as quickly as they were made. In time these papier-mâché tigers were given the name "little eat-'em-ups." This nickname was

In 1934, LSU students hoist their papier-mâché mascot onto the train before leaving to attend a game against Vanderbilt in Nashville.

Papier-mâché tigers, like this one created for the 1920 Arkansas football game, were destroyed almost as quickly as they were made.

*Clarence A. Ives Jr.*

apparently derived from an incident which occurred during an LSU-Tulane football game. Supposedly one of the LSU players attempted to bite off the ear of a Tulane player.

In 1924, an alumnus donated a small black South American cat, probably similar to a bobcat. He was named "Jerry," and he became LSU's first live mascot. Shortly after arrival his name was changed, as one might guess, to "Little Eat-'em-up." The cat was housed in the operating room of a local veterinarian, Dr. Prescott. Unfortunately, the football team lost all of its conference games that year, so "Little

Eat-'em-up" was sent away and the fans went back to using papier-mâché tigers from 1925 to 1936. While the paper tigers were good enough for some, others had a plan to bring a real symbol of the team's spirit to campus.

On January 1, 1936, the LSU Tigers played the TCU Horned Frogs in the Sugar Bowl. This illustration from *Pel-Mell* magazine predates the arrival of the live mascot to the LSU campus by less than a year.

*Courtesy Mrs. William Warren Munson*

# ── THEY WELCOME MIKE ──

◆ On Wednesday, Oct. 24th, the usually quiet campus of the Old War Skule was awakened by one of the most unusual and spontanous demonstration of spirit that has been shown in many years. In the early dawn, like a band of warring natives of the jungle attacking an unsuspecting village, the Students took complete control of the campus, turned out the classes, prevented professors and students with books from entering the campus and pronounced a holiday for President Smith, whether he wanted it or not. The procession then proceeded to the railroad station with the same enthusiasm to give their mascot, Old Mike, a young bengal tiger, as royal a reception as he could ever have received in the jungles of deepest India.

Exactly what this m a s c o t thought concerning the display of s p i r i t will never be known. Throughout the procession he remained calm as he was grand, surveying his new subjects with almost a look of approval.

Reading form left to right:

(1) The band in every day clothes leads the procession.

(2) Gathering around the gym.

(3) They turn out the Law school.

(4) They proceed to the campanile.

(5) Turning out the Music school.

(6) Procession passing t h e gym.

(7) Early dawn and the crowd gathers.

(8) No Profs—No School !

(9) No more law !

(10) The procession begins.

*Pel-Mell* issue showing the arrival of the first Bengal tiger to LSU's campus. The date of Mike's arrival is incorrectly listed as October 24.

*Courtesy Mrs. William Warren Munson*

# MIKE I, 1936–1956

It was early in the morning on Wednesday, October 21, 1936. The Cadet Corps and student body barred professors from their offices, picketed classrooms, and blocked all entrances to the campus. The band played underneath dormitory windows. According to Russell B. Long, freshmen class president and later United States senator, a few classes began but were quickly closed by students, causing President James M. Smith to declare a holiday and close the university. Just before noon, students paraded through Baton Rouge. Onlookers lined Highland Road, awaiting the entourage arriving from the train station. As the cavalcade approached, students swarmed around to get a look at the new arrival to the LSU family. In the evening they lit a bonfire

Mike with his keeper, ca. 1936.

and had a grand party. The band played all the versions they knew of "Tiger Rag." Newspapers recorded that Paris may have sung a welcome to General Pershing, New York may have

11

Mike arrives on October 21, 1936. Gumbo, *1937*

LSU's Head Athletic Trainer Mike Chambers visits his namesake in his first home at the Baton Rouge City Park Zoo. *Pop Strange*

Freshmen with strike signs picketed all entrances to campus on the day Mike arrived. Gumbo, *1937*

showered Charles Lindberg with ticker tape, but LSU students staged a campus strike equal to none to welcome their new tiger mascot to campus.

Two years earlier, in 1934, a decision had been made that would forever change life on the LSU campus. Head Athletic Trainer Chellis "Mike" Chambers, Athletic Director T. P. Heard, swimming pool manager and intramural swimming coach William G. "Hickey" Higginbotham, and LSU law student Ed Laborde decided to bring a real tiger to LSU, then known as the "Ole War Skule." They raised $750, collecting twenty-five cents from each student, and purchased a two-hundred-pound, one-year-old tiger from the Little Rock Zoo. They found him with the help of LSU student Ken Kavanaugh (later to become an All-American end), who had heard about a tiger being available from Little Rock and had notified Chambers. It seems that a circus tiger named Sheik had been banished to the Little Rock Zoo in 1928 after attacking a trainer. At the zoo Sheik was paired with a female tiger named Sue. Their cub was born on Thursday, October 10, 1935, and, like his father, was originally named Sheik. But his name was changed to Mike in honor of Chambers, the man most responsible for bringing him to LSU. Student body president Glen Olds had put the tiger name change to a vote of the student body, and it was overwhelmingly approved. Interestingly, Mike I must have remembered his original name because even years later Hickey Higginbotham could get him to roar just by calling "Sheik."

A portrait of Mike by the LSU Studio.

This is
*"Mike"*

Mascot for Louisiana State's
Tiger Football Team

COMPLIMENTS OF DALTON'S

## The Story of Mike

On Wednesday, October 24, 1936, the usually quiet campus of the Old War Skule was awakened by one of the most unusual and spontaneous demonstrations of spirit that has been shown in many years.

**MIKE CAME TO TOWN!**

Mike, the young bengal tiger, was born in Little Rock, Arkansas on October 10, 1935. He was purchased by the students through popular subscription and was named for Mike Chambers, L.S.U.'s trainer.

Each day, the mascot must have 10 or 12 pounds of fresh meat. In addition to this, on Monday his roast must have a coating of sulphur, which helps preserve the gloss of his royal coat.

On Wednesday, the steak must be garnished with a thick dope of salt to flavor the feline diet.

Every first and third Sunday, however, are Mike's big days. On these dates he receives two eggs and a pint of whole milk.

Mike will be taken to all important games on the team's schedule in his specially constructed trailer.

Card announcing the arrival of Mike on the LSU campus in 1936.

*Dr. Julie Schexnider*

Mike gets a new home near the football field.

*Elevation plan courtesy Somdal Associates*

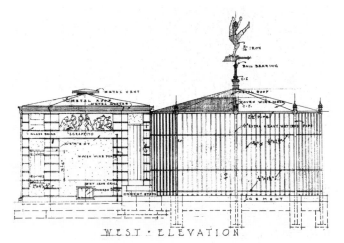

WEST ELEVATION

Mike I assumed his responsibilities just three days after arriving on campus. On October 24, 1936, Mike traveled to Shreveport to help LSU defeat Arkansas 19–7 under the leadership of team captain Bill May and Coach Bernie H. Moore. There was a rousing halftime show in Mike's honor and an increased excitement for LSU football that was noticeable to all. Mr. Gordon E. Doré, former member of the LSU Board of Supervisors, attended that first game. He said, "It was fantastic! It was during the depression days. Everyone needed

Mike's new home, completed in 1937.

anything that they could get to sort of pump them up a little bit. . . . The fact that our university was going to have a live tiger was absolutely fantastic! It was good for the university and good for the state. . . . It happened for the university and the state at a very special time." Throughout the day LSU fans chanted, "Let's feed the tiger a Razorback"! After such a wonderful initiation to LSU football, Mike began to travel with the team regularly.

When he wasn't traveling, Mike I stayed at the City Park Zoo under the care of the keeper, a Mr. Barry. The "zoo" was a small facility just north of the LSU campus, overlooking the LSU lakes. Mike quickly established a habit of rising at about 4:00 A.M. to roar a greeting to the new day. As a youngster, Mike I was a gentle tiger, regularly enjoying a lot of physical contact. That would change over time, as Mike reached adulthood. Although life was good at the zoo, Mike was moved down the hill onto the LSU campus after he got his leg and paw between the bars of his cage and slashed Higginbotham. A tiger house and a 27- by 34-foot outdoor cage were built next to the football stadium in 1937, at a cost of about $3,500. Mike's new home was dedicated by Governor Richard W. Leche prior to an LSU-Alabama baseball game on April 13 of that year. Records indicate that at the time, it cost about $600 per year to feed the tiger.

Governor Leche was a great fan of the new tiger. Richard W. Leche Jr. recalls a humorous conversation that took place in 1936 before an LSU football game, between the Governor and Porter "Eddie" Bryant. Bryant was a local vegetable vendor and LSU fan who claimed that his vegetables were "educated" because they were grown near the university. He therefore called himself the "Educated Vegetable Man." Shortly after Mike's arrival on campus, Bryant had named himself Mike's manager and regularly accompanied the tiger. While viewing Mike on the football field, the governor turned to Bryant and asked, "What will you do if he gets out of his cage?" Bryant quickly responded, "I'd get in it!"

From the beginning, Mike I was the

Mike speaks his mind on his eighteenth birthday, October 10, 1953.

Porter "Eddie" Bryant, known as "The Educated Vegetable Man," declared himself Mike's Head Keeper the day of Mike's arrival on campus.

Gumbo, *1937*

responsibility of the Athletic Department. For many years, Hickey Higginbotham had general oversight of Mike. Mike's day-to-day care was provided by students hired by the Athletic Department. In addition to a monthly salary, initially twenty-five dollars, students received a parking pass that allowed them to park by the Animal Science building where Mike's food was stored. They could also park near his cage. Even then, choice parking spots were highly coveted. Another bonus was getting to use a Ford convertible for the weekend.

Of course the car was to be used to pull Mike's trailer before the football games, but the students couldn't see any harm in putting a few miles on it over the weekend before returning it to the dealership.

Mike's first student caretakers were mem-

Auburn is the buggy,
Southwestern is the hoss,
Tulane did the driving,
For the Tigers is the boss.
—Porter "Eddie" Bryant,
1936

Mike plays with his keeper,
W. G. Higginbotham, ca.
1937.

*Leon Trice, Baton Rouge* Advocate

bers of the swimming and diving team. From the 1940s to the mid-1950s, the student care-taker position was passed down within the Sigma Chi fraternity and later through Theta Xi. Zeta Beta Tau fraternity, which is no longer active on the LSU campus, cared for Mike II and Mike III from 1957 until 1968. During much of the 1970s, two members of Kappa Sigma cared for Mike III and Mike IV. The lives of the many tiger "keepers" are themselves interesting stories. Many of them have

gone on to become successful professionals and businessmen. Charles Fourrier, Mike's keeper from 1939 to 1942, served in World War II and lost his life in an aircraft landing accident at Pearl Harbor. Osce R. Jones, a tiger keeper who became a P-51 fighter pilot, was shot down over France and spent time in a German POW camp.

Mike I attended football games as far away as Birmingham to help inspire the team to victory. Often he traveled by train, but usually he traveled in his $300 trailer, donated by the Louisiana Highway Department. During Mike's first few years as mascot, he traveled around the state in the summer as a publicity agent for the football team. He also accompanied the swim team occasionally as they traveled around Louisiana giving swimming and diving exhibitions and helping to dedicate new swimming pool facilities. In 1949, relates former LSU swimmer Fred Frey Jr., when Hickey Higginbotham and members of the LSU swim team were returning from an event near Lake Charles they stopped at a gas station in the town of Kinder. Of course the live tiger immediately drew a crowd. Higginbotham joked to the gathering onlookers that it was "time to let Mike out for a walk." The local sheriff, who was in the crowd, reached for his

Governor Richard W. Leche (*foreground*) on the field with Mike, ca. 1936. To his left is Lt. Gov. Earl K. Long.

*Richard W. Leche Papers, MSS 2060, LLMV Collections, LSU Libraries, Baton Rouge*

Morning Advocate
**Magazine Section**

Sunday October 23, 1949

The Sunday *Morning Advocate* Magazine Section cover featured Mike in his favorite pose in 1949.

car towing him. That happened on at least two separate occasions during parades down Third Street in Baton Rouge. In both cases, a group of coed cheerleaders were sitting up on the back seat of the towing car, a convertible, when all of a sudden they started screaming and diving for cover. Both Hickey Higginbotham and Jere D. Melilli would later laugh about it, but at the time they didn't dare!

During his tenure, Mike I eventually traveled to all of the schools in the Southeastern Conference. Occasionally, Mike and Higginbotham would get back into Baton Rouge after midnight. Rather than going to the trouble of returning Mike to his enclosure at such an hour, Higginbotham would park Mike's trailer inside his garage at home. The neighbors got used to hearing the sounds of a tiger coming from the Higginbotham garage!

It seems that once Mike I even got a nighttime tour of parts of Baton Rouge, courtesy of his student caretakers. According to Gordon Doré, Mike's keepers loaded him up and took him into town one night, making sure that people saw the tiger in his trailer. Then they returned to campus and quickly unloaded him. When they returned to the same parts of town with the trailer empty and the gate swinging open, they got an entirely different response. People were convinced that the tiger was loose in their neighborhood, and many went scurrying for the safety of their homes.

gun and said, "If you let that tiger out, y'all are going to jail!"

Mike I was unusual for a tiger in that he liked to stand up in his trailer while traveling. This was sometimes a problem, since he could spray urine right into the seats of the

20

Homecoming trophies adorn the top of Mike's trailer in 1942.

*Courtesy Mrs. Osce R. Jones*

The students encouraged the deception by asking people if they'd seen the tiger. The story goes that parts of the city closed up early that night!

Mike I ate a hearty daily meal of eight to twelve pounds of meat, sometimes covered with cod-liver oil, a slab of salt, and often, as a special treat, three eggs and a quart of milk to maintain his sleek coat. Several have said that Mike I would refuse to eat if he were being watched. Of course during World War II Mike's allotment of meat was rationed like everyone else's. He did not like this one bit. Former students living in the stadium dormitories at the time have told of Mike keeping them

Mississippi State University mascot Bully meets Mike.

*Courtesy of the Mississippi State University Libraries, University Archives*

A view of the tiger's cage taken from North Stadium dormitory, ca. 1945. During the war, Mike kept many a stadium dorm student awake with his protests for more food.

*Courtesy Frank M. O'Quinn*

awake at night with his roaring. Anyone who has heard a tiger roar can imagine how difficult it would be to go to sleep with that terrifying sound. There was even a plan to transport Mike to the Audubon Zoo for the duration of the war so that he would have access to adequate food. LSU students were not very excited about seeing their beloved mascot housed in Tulane territory. Some students even forced student body president Hugh O'Connor and vice president Jeff Burkett to ride around campus on parade in Mike's trailer, pulled by seven male students, prior to a meeting with university officials to discuss the transfer. Finally, with so much opposition from the student body the plans to ship Mike to New Orleans were scrapped.

When fully grown, Mike I was of average size at 450 pounds. Mike definitely had some dislikes. Although he enjoyed cooling off in his water trough, several caretakers recall that he became very agitated when sprayed with a hose. Neither was Mike I overly fond of people, as several of his caretakers would later attest. Eddy Contine, one of Mike's early student caretakers, once found himself face-to-face with the tiger. Contine had forgotten to close a gate before entering his enclosure. He was so frightened, all he could stutter was: "Hic . . . Hic . . . Hickey!" Hickey Higginbotham grabbed a pan and started running it along the cage, calling out, "Sheik!" That distracted Mike long enough for the terrified student to make his escape. Similar near catastrophes

Mike enjoys a hearty meal in 1941.

*Courtesy Mrs. Osce R. Jones*

Students in 1946 hold up the traditional "Rag" claimed each year by the winner of the LSU-Tulane football game, an annual rivalry at that time.

*Courtesy University Relations*

occurred when Mike's next caretakers, Charles Fourrier and Osce R. Jones, on separate occasions, mistakenly forgot to close the gate separating themselves from Mike. Fortunately for all, they managed to escape from the cage before Mike decided to attack. A few years later, Brittain Briggs once got too close to the cage while chipping ice off the lock. Seeing the opportunity, Mike reached a paw through the bars and slapped Briggs to the ground with one swat. Later, former LSU student Bob Bogan recalls accompanying Mike

to Austin for a game against the University of Texas. Bogan made the mistake of putting his finger into Mike's cage. Mike promptly bit it, sending Bogan on a trip to the local hospital. The attending physician wouldn't believe his story until it was confirmed by another physician who happened to be an LSU graduate and assured him that, yes, LSU did own a tiger. Bogan wasn't the first to have such a close call with Mike. Jere Melilli's brush with Mike was even closer. He recalls a time when he was inside Mike's house trying to coax him

Cheerleaders in 1950 pump up the fans from atop Mike's cage.

car, a 1941 Studebaker. Jere could squeak that door from a hundred yards away, and that was enough to get the tiger fighting mad.

Mike I doesn't seem to have been too fond of other animals either. At least he kept up the age-old conflict between cats and dogs, and this time the cats won. Jere Melilli recalls a time when he had just opened the door into Mike's house, and out of nowhere a very small dog ran past him and right up to Mike. Melilli watched in horror as Mike reached through the bars and pulled the dog in with him in one fell swoop. Melilli says that in a matter of seconds all that was left of the dog was his collar and a few tufts of hair. Mike had made a snack of him! That and the shoe-slashing incident served as permanent reminders to Melilli of just how fast, powerful, and dangerous these animals are.

Mike I had almost as eventful a life as Mike IV would have forty years later. At least twice, in 1941 and 1953, students threw birthday parties for Mike. In 1941 a musical revue, "Hold That Tiger" was scheduled to coincide with a rally for the LSU–Texas A&M game. Of course Mike was the guest of honor. During the show about 150 Aggies tried to break up the party but were thwarted by LSU cadets. Then, in 1953, the student body declared the weekend of Saturday, October 10, "Mike's Birthday Party." The theme of the party was, "Knock out Kentucky for the love of Mike." A

out, when his foot slipped toward Mike. In an instant, Mike reached through the bars and slashed Melilli's shoe. There is no doubt that Mike was trying to get the student's foot inside the cage. Confirming that Mike I did not care much for his keepers, Melilli recalls how Mike knew the sound of the squeaky door on his

Mike pins back his ears in response to something that has upset him.

large birthday cake, complete with peppermint goalposts and over a thousand candle "spectators," was made and generously donated by Mr. Jack Sabin, owner of The Goal Post, a local restaurant. Of course in a bottom layer of the cake was a raw roast for Mike. The celebration was campuswide and included the football coaches and team, the Tiger band, the Purple Jackets, the Pershing Rifles, the Cadet Corps, and several dormitory groups. In spite of all the hoopla, the game ended in a 6–6 tie.

In 1944 alumnus and former LSU track star Lieutenant Alfred M. L. "Smokey" Sanders and crew intended to honor Mike by having his name and picture painted on the nose of their B-24 bomber. Above Mike's name and image was also to be painted *The Spirit of LSU,* the name Sanders gave the plane. The bomber was proudly flown in many combat missions over Europe during World War II and was the only aircraft of WWII named after Louisiana State University. Mission records reveal

This poster of *The Spirit of LSU* was painted in the 1970s using Mike III's image.

*Painting by Glenn Gore*

The only known photograph of *The Spirit of LSU*.

that *The Spirit of LSU* was often the formation leader. Unfortunately, the crew never got the opportunity to have Mike's image painted on the plane. On May 28, 1944, just nine days before D day, Sanders was to take the *Spirit* on another mission, but because the bomber was known as one of the fastest in the squadron,

A scaled-down replica of part of a B-24 Liberator flown by LSU alumnus Alfred M. L. "Smokey" Sanders. Sanders' crew planned to have a picture of Mike the Tiger, along with the words "Mike—The Spirit of LSU," painted on the forward fuselage, but the aircraft was shot down over Belgium before the artwork could be applied. A replica of the intended artwork was recently produced in tribute to Sanders and his crew and is shown here. *Ginger Guttner*

The crew of *The Spirit of LSU* (Lieutenant Sanders standing far left).

another officer pulled rank and took the aircraft instead. Sanders was assigned a slower bomber for the day's mission. On that day, Sanders and his crew were hit by flak while on a bombing run over Germany. In spite of heavy damage to his ship, Sanders managed to release his bombs and turned back toward England. Not able to make it across the channel, all the crew members bailed out, and the aircraft crashed in Belgium. Sanders was captured, but he escaped with help from Belgian nationals. He returned to England on September 9, 1944. Sanders' love for LSU was shared by his young bride Mildred ("Millie"), also an LSU graduate. Millie learned of her husband's capture just days after their son was born. Not knowing whether she would see her tiger again, she named their son "Mike."

As Mike I passed middle age, many were concerned that time was growing short for him to sire a cub. After all, he would eventually need an heir. Two attempts were made to send him on a quest for love at the Audubon Zoo. However, in each case the LSU student body blocked the efforts. They did not relish the idea of their beloved mascot going to New Orleans. The Crescent City was considered hostile territory, home to arch rival Tulane. Finally, in July 1945, the student body agreed by a vote of 403 to 4 that Mike should travel to

Lieutenant Alfred M. L. "Smokey" Sanders intended to have a picture of Mike painted on the nose of his B-24 bomber, dubbed *The Spirit of LSU.*

the R. M. Taylor Zoo in Jackson, Mississippi. Awaiting him there was a lovely three-and-a-half-year-old female tiger named Desdemona.

E. L. Upp, an LSU cheerleader and Mike's student caretaker at the time, went along on the trip to Mississippi. Quite a stir was caused everywhere they stopped along the way. At one gas station in Mississippi, Mike sprayed a little boy all dressed up in his Sunday best who had come out to see him. The shocked boy ran off to tell his mother. One can imagine her disbelief when he told her he was sprayed by a tiger!

Once unloaded from his trailer at the zoo, Mike immediately began to get nervous, perhaps because of the strange environment or because he sensed the female nearby. Eventually the two tigers, separated by some fencing, sighted one another. Desdemona saw Mike first and gave out a snort and a growl. But instead of returning the greeting, Mike jumped back in such fear that he landed flat on his back. LSU staff were concerned that the Ole Miss faithful would find out about the incident and use it mockingly to their advantage. Fortunately, word didn't get out that Mike was afraid of a female tiger. Though Mike stayed at the Jackson zoo for a few months, he and Desdemona never really hit it off, and he eventually returned without having had the opportunity to breed. It was feared that the risk of injury to one or both of the tigers was too great to allow contact.

When LSU traveled to the January 1, 1947, Cotton Bowl, Hickey Higginbotham hitched Mike's cage to his car and headed for Dallas. When they left Baton Rouge it was 85 degrees and sunny. When they reached Shreveport it was 15 degrees and sleeting. Not wanting to expose Mike to more inclement weather, Higginbotham got permission from Alfred Glassell to shelter Mike in his warehouse for a few days. Unfortunately, the night watchman wasn't told of Mike's arrival. When the poor man entered the warehouse on his nightly

rounds and shined his flashlight on Mike, the tiger let out a growl that nearly scared the man to death. It is rumored that the man never completely recovered from the experience.

On December 1, 1950, one of the most famous episodes in the history of the tiger mascots occurred. The most reliable account of the incident comes from Tom Freeman, who frequently assisted Mike's caretaker David Melilli. It came about when Mike I was taken to New Orleans for a game against Tulane. It was customary when traveling to New Orleans for a football game for Mike to avoid the Saturday traffic by arriving a day early. Mike would frequently stay at Ye Olde College Inn, under the eye of a night watchman. On this occasion, the watchman went to the rear of the inn to find a tarpaulin to cover the trailer. Melilli, who had gone to the Roosevelt Hotel, returned to the inn about ten minutes later, only to find Mike missing! He then woke Freeman, and the two of them drove around New Orleans listening for a tiger's roar. What they didn't know was that Mike had been hidden in the Tulane football stadium and was being guarded by Tulane students and local police. The plan hatched by the Tulane students was for their cheerleaders to return Mike to the LSU cheerleaders at halftime. When Melilli and Freeman found Mike, they attempted to retrieve their precious mascot, but the police would not give him up. Finally, at literally the last hour, LSU athletic director T. P. "Red" Heard demanded Mike's return. He was reluctantly handed over. The LSU students had just enough time to remove the blue and green crepe streamers from the trailer as Mike was entering the stadium. Unfortunately, there was no time to remove the green paint from the trailer, where the Tulane tigernappers had proudly announced the name of the offending university. This incident served to fuel the rivalry between the schools for many years.

In his many travels, Mike I miraculously survived at least two automobile accidents. The most serious occurred on November 25, 1951, on U.S. Highway 71, about fifteen miles north of Coushatta, Louisiana. Mike was returning

in triumph from a 45–7 victory over Villanova in Shreveport. A motorist drove onto the highway shoulder and attempted to pass Mike's trailer. Caretaker David Melilli, who was towing Mike's trailer at the time, was himself trying to pass a slower vehicle. Melilli swerved back into his lane, but in the process Mike's trailer flipped over into a ditch. Fortunately, nobody, including Mike, was injured. A wrecker from Coushatta was called out and righted the trailer. After clearance from state trooper E. C. Clinton, the entourage was on its way again.

In 1953, Mike I was ceremonially honored with a varsity letter from Kenner Day, then national president of the L Club. Also in 1953, university officials decided that, due to advancing age, Mike's traveling days were over. Unfortunately, that policy appears not to have been followed completely. On November 27, 1954, Mike was once again on his way to New Orleans for the LSU-Tulane game. A sudden stop by his caretaker, Bob Dodwell, caused Mike's trailer to jackknife and turn over on Airline Highway. Although Dodwell was slightly injured, Mike was once again unharmed.

In 1955, the aged Mike I became ill. Dr. Joe Dixon of the LSU Department of Veterinary Science was asked by golf coach Harry Taylor to provide veterinary care for the tiger. Thereafter, while the Athletic Department retained

Mike I and coed Betty Ann Landry.

*Courtesy University Relations*

authority over the tiger's day-to-day life, Mike I and subsequent tigers would have a veterinarian to attend to their medical needs. This was a significant advance in the overall care of the LSU tiger mascots.

Mike I died on Friday, June 29, 1956, of complications associated with kidney disease. In backyards all over Louisiana, children held mock funerals in his honor. Others hung his photograph, draped in black crepe paper. Many people who had been present on campus at his arrival or had grown up visiting him mourned his passing. He was twenty years and eight months old at his death and had reigned at LSU for nearly twenty years. Without a doubt Mike I created a legacy in which Mike the Tiger has come to symbolize the heart and soul of LSU athletics.

Mike I began a long tradition as a proud symbol of LSU, and he was featured in numerous publications, including Paul D. Buchanan's *Famous Animals of the States.* Following Mike's death, a fund was established to perpetuate his memory by mounting his pelt in a lifelike manner and displaying him at the university's Louisiana Museum of Natural History. Museum taxidermist P. A. Daigre oversaw the painstaking process. Mike I remains proudly displayed in the museum to this day, the patriarch of a long and great LSU tradition. Now, however, he is part of a tiger education exhibit created and installed in 2011.

After his death, the university's Louisiana Museum of Natural History's taxidermist P. A. Daigre oversaw the painstaking process of mounting Mike's pelt in a lifelike pose.

*Courtesy University Relations*

## MIKE I'S STUDENT CARETAKERS

1936–37: L. C. Aycock

1937–38: Preston Vallas

1938  39: Elliot"Eddy" Contine

1939–42: Charles Fourrier

1942–43: Osce R. Jones

1943–44: Charles Upp

1944–45: George Thompson

1945–46: E. Loy Upp

1946–47: H. Staton Barlow

1947–49: Brittain Briggs

1949–51: David Melilli

1951–53: Jere D. Melilli

1953–55: Bob Dodwell

1955–56: Gene Smith

Mike II was six months old
when this picture was taken
by Bob Morgan.

# MIKE II, 1956-1958

On July 1, 1956, just a few days after the death of the beloved Mike I, Representative Kenneth Deshotel of St. Landry introduced a resolution in the Louisiana legislature endorsing the purchase of another tiger. The resolution also conveyed sympathy to the LSU community for the loss of Mike I. Deshotel stated that he hoped that the new tiger would be called "Mike II." On campus, the Mike the Tiger Fund was launched by student body president Enos Parker and fellow students Vic Koepp and John Nunn to purchase "Mike Junior." Students away from campus for the summer were encouraged to mail in their contributions. It was hoped that a new tiger could be found by the start of the next football season. The first game was scheduled for September 29

Coeds collect money to purchase a new tiger.

The first Mike II was chosen over his littermate because of his larger paws.

would come equally from student fees and the Athletic Department. This was an important step toward assuring proper care of Mike II as well as his successors.

To this day the story of Mike II remains shrouded in mystery. Mike II was born on February 28, 1956, at the Audubon Zoo in New Orleans. He was the son of a four-year-old male named Jim, originally from the Cincinnati Zoo. His mother was a lovely five-year-old tiger named Carol, who had some circus experience. Mike II was one of two tiger cubs being considered for sale to LSU by the Audubon Zoo. He was selected because his paws were larger than those of the other cub. Mike II arrived secretly on the LSU campus on September 28, 1956. The young tiger was held overnight in the football stadium, guarded in two-hour shifts by members of the student council against any would-be Tulane pranksters. The tiger sitters included Don Lartigue, Fred Hartdegan, Ed Thornhill, Laurie Sledge, John Nunn, and Tom Young. Mike's unveiling occurred the next day, September 29, opening day of the new football season. An academic holiday was declared, and the celebrations began. A parade led by the LSU band wound through downtown Baton Rouge. Parade participants decorated their cars with streamers and signs bearing slogans such as "I Like Mike" and "Dig That Crazy Cat." Later, there was a general campus open house, a drill

against the Aggies of Texas A&M. There wasn't much time, but the money was quickly raised. On August 4, the LSU Board of Supervisors passed a resolution stating that caretaker salaries and maintenance costs for the new tiger

Local banking institutions issued tiger banks like the one above to customers upon the birth of children in their family during the late 1950s.

This tiger child's bank is from a Shreveport bank.

A parade led by the LSU band was held in downtown Baton Rouge to celebrate the arrival of the new Mike.

The Lambda Chi Alpha float
in Mike's parade.

*Courtesy University Relations*

routine, a salute by the Pershing Rifles, and a welcoming ceremony honoring the new, regal addition to the LSU family. During the ceremony, a check for $1,500 was presented to George Douglas, superintendent of the Audubon Zoo, by Enos Parker. Several persons who had played prominent roles in the life of Mike I returned to campus to honor his heir. Among them were two former cheerleaders, sisters Juliette and Marie Louise Bonnette;

former athletic trainer Mike Chambers; 1936 student body president Glen Olds; and former traveling companion of Mike I, Ed Laborde. In the evening there were parties in Mike's honor.

Legend has it that less than a month after his arrival at LSU, Mike II died of pneumonia at only eight months of age during a six-game losing streak. Reportedly, Mike II was then secretly buried under a willow tree along the Mississippi River by newly appointed

A young Mike II chews on a football. A color version of this image first appeared on the cover of *Dixie Roto* magazine on October 21, 1956.

*Philip Guarisco,* © 1956 New Orleans Times-Picayune

athletic director Jim Corbett, campus police chief C. R. "Dick" Anderson, and LSU Athletic Department business manager Jack Gilmore. According to Gilmore, a campus police officer found the tiger dead at 1:00 A.M. that October morning. Jim Corbett was immediately called in. Inside the tiger cage, reflecting on the gravity of the situation, Corbett said to others on the scene, "I can see the newspaper stories now. The football team is so bad that even the tiger couldn't bear the shame." To explain Mike's absence, a statement was issued

The second Mike II.

*Courtesy Chico Moore*

in the LSU *Daily Reveille* on October 23 saying that Mike was having trouble adjusting to his enclosure and was therefore being kept inside "until he becomes more accustomed to the excitement of being a mascot." Jim Corbett Jr., eleven years old at the time, says that his father never told him what happened next, but he recalls phone calls being made in a frantic effort to find another tiger. It was Jack Gilmore who located a cub of the right age at the Woodland

In this photo, a young Mike
II has not yet developed his
adult canine teeth.

Gumbo, *1958*

Cheerleaders on the brand new "tiger chariot," custom-built for Mike, ca. 1957.

Cheerleaders from the 1956 football season ride the top of the original trailer.

Gumbo, *1957*

Park Zoo in Seattle. Gilmore says that he arranged for the cub to be delivered to the Audubon Zoo in New Orleans.

In addition to Gilmore's testimony, several pieces of evidence support the legend that the original Mike II died and was replaced by another young tiger. However, few of these facts were widely known at the time. Records from the Woodland Park Zoo in Seattle do list a litter of three cubs born February 24, 1956, almost the same date as the tiger born at Audubon Zoo. There is no record of

Tulane Green Wave graffiti on Mike's home from the 1956 football season is painted over, under the watchful eyes of several disgruntled LSU students.
Gumbo, *1957*

what became of those cubs. It is certainly possible that one of those cubs was brought to LSU from Seattle via New Orleans and given the name Mike II. Records from the Audubon Zoo for 1956 refer to a tiger cub being purchased from the Seattle zoo and transferred to Baton Rouge. Photographs of Mike II taken before and after his convalescence are clearly of two different tigers. Careful examination reveals that while very similar, the facial markings of the two tigers, unique as human fingerprints, are indeed different. When Mike II

Mike II snarls and reveals that his canine teeth have grown larger and more robust.

A wreath is hung by SGA vice president Mippy Jackson to mourn the death of the second tiger on the LSU campus.

*Courtesy University Relations*

was once again allowed to leave his tiger house that November, he seemed to have grown at a tremendous rate. Various records from the time list Mike's weight at 65 pounds in September 1956 and 130 pounds by November 28. There is even record of a necropsy (an autopsy of an animal) being performed on a tiger cub at a medical center in New Orleans during the time that Mike was supposedly being kept in isolation. Nevertheless, all rumors of the death

and replacement of Mike II were denied. The official story was that Mike II had finally adjusted to life as a mascot, that he was in great health, and that the necropsied cub was actually Mike's litter mate.

The second Mike II (if indeed there was a "phoney feline") reigned at LSU for only one season. He died at the Audubon Zoo on May 15, 1958, of complications associated with multiple fractures to his left rear leg. It was not known exactly how or when the leg was injured. There was speculation that the injury occurred when he jumped from a pedestal in his cage to the concrete floor below, and the injury is known to have occurred sometime near the end of the previous September. Mike was taken to the Audubon Zoo in April for treatment of the leg, but an uncontrollable infection arose.

Mike was taken to Charity Hospital in New Orleans for a necropsy. Maxine Marionneaux, a medical technology student at the hospital, tells of finding Mike II on a table in the morgue. Maxine, who worked in the emergency room laboratory next door, had gone to the morgue in the middle of the night to use the phone. Marionneaux recalls, "When I walked into the morgue, there was that huge tiger laid out on that table. At the time, it wasn't funny. I couldn't believe it." She'd been exposed to some unusual things in the morgue but never a tiger!

Despite his death at a young age, at least one very positive development came during Mike II's short reign. In September, 1957, a brand new, custom-built "tiger chariot" was purchased. It was built by Sam Miley of Miley Horse Trailers in Fort Worth, Texas. This "tiger taxi" replaced the much smaller and less stable cage that had been used to transport Mike I and Mike II. The new trailer would serve as the traveling cage for Mike II and his successors until 1997, when it was replaced after forty years of service. The design of the trailer was so good that few modifications were made in the construction of the 1997 model.

## MIKE II'S STUDENT CARETAKERS

1956–57: Gene Smith

1957–58: Sidney S. Miller

1958: Bill Levenson

The second Mike II appeared
on this color poster, ca. 1957.

*Erby M. Aucoin Jr.*

Mike III in 1968.

# MIKE III, 1958–1976

Just in time for the national championship football season of 1958, Jim Corbett and Jack Gilmore located and purchased Mike III, coincidentally, from the Seattle zoo. This new mascot was born on Tuesday, November 26, 1957, and arrived at LSU in late August 1958. The LSU student body raised $1,500 for his purchase and transportation (though the final purchase price was only $950, with an additional $100 for transportation). Mike III was flown to Chicago on "Flying Tiger Airlines," then on to New Orleans on Delta Airlines. A five-cent "tradition fee" was assessed each student for the tiger's care. Mike III was introduced to the general public at the first home game of the 1958 season, on October 4 against Hardin-Simmons University. LSU won 20–6.

Raising funds again for Mike.

*Baton Rouge* Advocate

Mike III in the fall of 1959. The photographer bravely entered Mike's outer cage and was fine until the caretaker got Mike to roar (*left*). When the flash went off, Mike stared straight at the photographer and roared even louder. The photographer was terrified, but the shot was worth it: the official tiger logo still in use today was copied from the resulting photo (*right*).

*Erby M. Aucoin Jr.*

According to Mike III's first student caretaker, Bill Levenson, the new mascot adjusted easily to life at LSU. Mike III lived a long and healthy life on about twelve pounds of horsemeat per day along with cod-liver oil, vitamins, and minerals. Mike was also regularly given freshly killed chickens, which Dr. Dixon had heard were good for tigers. Though Mike III's long life was relatively uneventful, it was not completely without incident. He broke both rear legs shortly after arrival at LSU, probably while jumping onto the hard cage floor. Fortunately, he was laid up for only six weeks, and the limbs healed quickly under Dr.

Dixon's care. Douglas Davidson, Mike's caretaker from 1959 to 1961, and his friend and assistant Howard Dumont report that before one LSU-Tulane football game, some Tulane students threw green paint all over Mike. Dr. Dixon, with the help of several student assistants, anesthetized Mike and examined him to determine whether he had ingested any of the paint. Fortunately, it appeared that he had not. After that incident the caretakers would lock Mike up for up to a week before the LSU-Tulane football game to protect him from pranksters. Otherwise, student caretakers from the era report that Mike III was rarely ill and required very little veterinary care. He did need a root canal procedure at one time, but he appeared to have weathered that well. Also, according to Joel Samuels, Mike's caretaker from 1965 to 1968, the surface of his outer enclosure had been coated with a purple and gold rubberized material that prevented his claws from wearing normally. As a result, Mike's claws would overgrow and had to be trimmed by Dr. Dixon every six months. After

Dr. William Oglesby (*left,* then head of the Veterinary Science Department), Dr. Joe Dixon (*center*), and Dr. Robert Lank put casts on Mike's broken legs.

*Baton Rouge* Advocate

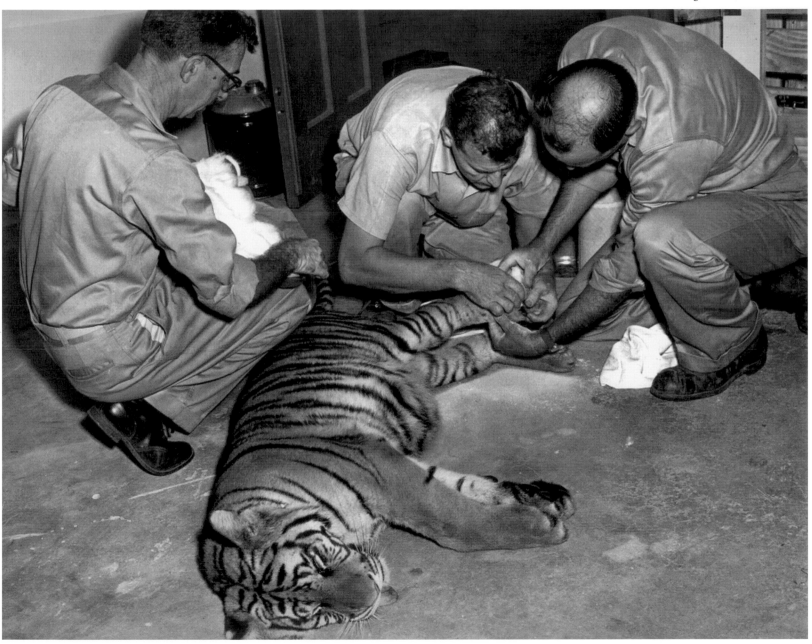

one particularly bothersome overgrown nail was removed, the new floor was too. Mike III was a very hearty tiger. On at least one occasion temperatures dropped to fourteen degrees inside his tiger house, freezing his water. Although he seemed to tolerate it well, a kerosene heater was quickly added to warm things up a bit, and fresh water was brought in regularly until the cold snap ended.

It was apparent to his keepers early on that Mike III was a much calmer tiger than Mike II (either of them!) had been. His calm nature may have saved the lives of at least four of his keepers. The first was Alvin Meyer Jr., Mike's

student caretaker from 1961 to 1963. One day he forgot to make sure that Mike was safely locked in his tiger house before he went in to clean the enclosure. Going about his business, Meyer came face-to-face with the big cat. Mike had wandered out of his house looking for his twelve pounds of horsemeat. Fortunately for all, he was more interested in his supper than he was in the student. Needless to say, Meyer beat a hasty retreat to allow Mike to dine alone. Meyer had another brush with disaster when Mike grabbed Meyer's foot with his paw. Meyer was sitting in the tiger house with his feet propped up against the cage bars

John Korver works on the well-known illustration of Mike coming out of Tiger Stadium, 1960.

*Courtesy University Relations*

Mike III interacts with someone kneeling outside of his cage.

*Courtesy Joel Samuels*

when Mike decided to play with Meyer's leg. Of course after that Meyer decided he'd better keep his feet a bit further from the cage.

Joel Samuels reports that on at least three occasions, he accidentally entered the enclosure thinking that Mike was locked up when he wasn't. In two of Samuels' narrow escapes from the cage, Mike jumped up on the cage door just after the fleeing student closed it behind him. Bob Lank Jr., Mike's caretaker from 1968 to 1972, develops sweaty palms and a quickening pulse when he recalls the time he too found himself in the cage with Mike III. Lank was cleaning up in the outer enclosure when a bystander asked why Mike didn't attack him. He confidently replied, "Because

of that gate." When the woman asked "What gate?" he turned to find that he had forgotten to lower the gate that locked Mike inside his tiger house. Fortunately, Mike was calmly

The Tiger Train, used to transport students from outlying parking lots to the center of campus, ran from 1963 until 1970.

Mike III greets visitors in 1964.

eating his dinner and didn't notice the frightened student as he dashed out of the enclosure to safety. Lank was terribly shaken up by the experience. In fact, he was so frightened that it took a few days for him to settle down.

Philip Aman, Mike's caretaker in the spring of 1972, recalls a similar experience. He had entered Mike's enclosure to clean up, forgetting to lock the tiger inside his house while the hungry cat ate his supper. Aman was in the process of hosing down the enclosure when he noticed his potentially fatal error. He realized that he had to make his escape before Mike noticed him. The only problem was having to cross in front of the open gate of Mike's house. Having to choose between a risky escape and certain danger once Mike finished his dinner, Aman made a dash for the outer gate. As he rushed by the open door, he startled Mike, who turned only in time to see the student reach safety. After composing himself, Aman dropped the gate, locking Mike in the house, and returned to his duties inside the enclosure.

Paul Marks Jr., Mike's caretaker from 1963 to 1965 recalls that once in the early sixties when LSU was to play Ole Miss, it was rumored that the Ole Miss fans were planning a caper the night before the game. It seems they planned to paint whatever they could find, including Mike III if possible, red and blue. The campus police encouraged Marks to spend the night guarding Mike's cage. That did not seem like the best idea to a student who liked his sleep. So Mike was loaded into his trailer for a trip to the home of Marks's parents. There he spent a peaceful night in a closed garage, safe from any would be Picassos from Mississippi. And the student got his good night's sleep!

Because LSU competed in so many bowl games during the reign of Mike III, his caretakers have many stories to tell of their travels. Joel Samuels tells of taking Mike III to

The new tiger suit is introduced in 1959.

*Courtesy University Relations*

Dallas for the Cotton Bowl of 1966, when LSU was pitted against the Razorbacks of Arkansas. Though a two-touchdown underdog, LSU won the game 14–7. Afterward, at the Cotton Bowl banquet, the governors of Louisiana, Arkansas, and Texas were deeply engrossed in conversation with one another. When Samuels was introduced as "the Tiger Man," all three governors stopped their conversation and turned their attention to him. Each was more interested in talking about Mike than in talking to one another. Samuels also recalls an LSU-Alabama game when Bear Bryant was the Alabama head coach. Samuels had a way of getting Mike to growl simply by saying, "Get 'em Mike." As the Alabama players gathered around the tiger trailer, Samuels quietly gave Mike the signal to growl. When Mike did so, it so unnerved the Alabama players that Coach Bryant took Samuels aside and gave him a stern lecture, advising him in no uncertain terms that he was not to upset his players like that. As far as we know, none of the other tigers growled on verbal cue.

Dr. Dixon continued to care for Mike III as the tiger aged. During the late 1960s and into the 1970s, he was assisted by his colleague Dr. Donald Gene Luther, who routinely checked on Mike to make sure he was well cared for. Often, Dr. Luther was the veterinarian who would accompany Mike into Tiger Stadium prior to the football games, an event just as exciting then as it is now. The tiger crew would load Mike into his trailer and pull him into the southeast corner of the stadium. The LSU cheerleaders would then climb up on top of Mike's trailer. As they started to round the stadium, the crowd would erupt with cheering. The excitement and the noise were so great once that Dr. Luther's young son, Marty, commented he could not hear himself scream! The crew would bring Mike to a stop and unload the cheerleaders in front of the student

Alabama coach "Bear" Bryant gets friendly with Mike in this photo taken in 1981 at Legion Field in Birmingham. Bryant was not so happy with Mike III's ability to roar on cue when he did so near the Alabama football players at an earlier time in Tiger Stadium.

*Tim Statum*

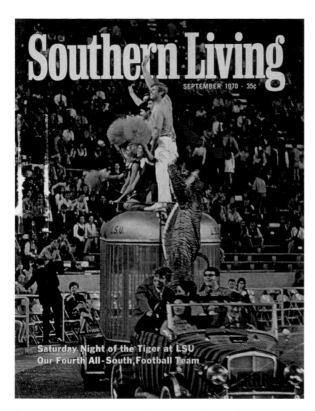

September 1970 issue of *Southern Living* features the roadster painted in a tiger motif.

*1970 Southern Living, Inc. Reprinted with permission.*

section, and the volume would increase even more. Dr. Luther recalled an occasion when he was standing next to the trailer, helping the cheerleaders to dismount, when one of the male cheerleaders banged on the trailer, causing the big cat to charge forward. As he did, he let out the most furious roar the veterinarian had ever heard. To him, Mike's canine teeth looked as big as telephone posts. It was the first time Dr. Luther fully appreciated Mike's great strength and quickness. It has been many years since the cheerleaders banged on Mike's

trailer, but that was how he was made to roar at the time.

The tiger trailer was usually pulled by a Ford Fairlane convertible provided by Richards Ford. Joel Samuels reports that in the 1960s, he would sometimes be loaned the next year's Ford model to pull the trailer. These models were so new that many fans were seeing them for the first time. In 1968, an LSU fan from Florida donated a roadster painted in a tiger motif. The car was used to tow the tiger trailer before the football games. Bob Lank Jr.,

Cheerleaders dismount the trailer.

Trailer being pulled in Tiger Stadium by a Ford Fairlane convertible.

*Courtesy Joel Samuels*

Mike III in 1968.

Mike's caretaker at the time, reports that while the roadster was certainly beautiful, he was very disappointed at losing the convertible. He had been looking forward to using that car on the weekends when not pulling Mike. He says that the roadster was very difficult to maneuver within the stadium and would frequently overheat. After the 1972 season, the tiger keepers retired the roadster and began using trucks to pull the trailer.

Mike III stopped traveling with the football team in 1972 when his trailer overturned on Highway 190 en route to a fund-raising event in Shreveport. Randy Kilgore was not driving on that trip but was along for the ride as Mike's student caretaker. He reports that the accident occurred because an incorrectly sized

A 1970 illustration of Mike.
*Courtesy Thomas Todd*

all future tigers whenever they left campus. That policy remains in force to this day.

It was in 1976 that Dr. W. Sheldon Bivin of the LSU School of Veterinary Medicine was asked to take over as veterinarian for Mike III. Dr. Bivin was head of both the Division of Laboratory Animal Medicine and the exotic animal medicine service in the School of Veterinary Medicine. He was therefore the natural choice to become Mike's next veterinarian. This marked the formal transfer of responsibility for the tiger from the Athletic Department to a veterinarian. Mike was quite old at the time and was experiencing more frequent age-related health problems. These problems included painful, degenerative bone changes that made walking and even eating difficult.

Mike's home in 1975 when students began to raise money to enlarge and improve the 39-year-old cage.
*Baton Rouge* Advocate

ball had been installed on the towing vehicle. When the trailer hit a bump in the highway, it bounced clear of the towing vehicle, ran into the median at forty-five miles per hour, flipped twice, and collided with a tractor-trailer rig. Amazingly, Mike escaped with only a small wound on one paw. Traffic backed up for miles. Police from seven different units arrived on the scene, along with a police helicopter. The trailer sustained so much damage that Mike had to be freed from it by cutting the door off with a torch. After that incident it was decided that a police escort should accompany

Menacing Mike III in cage.

*Courtesy Joel Samuels*

It was suggested by some that Mike be humanely put to sleep, but others did not believe that was fitting for an LSU mascot, and so Mike lived on for a short while. It was during the latter part of Mike III's life that student attitudes toward keeping a tiger captive in a small enclosure began to change. Efforts were begun to provide Mike with a larger, more natural enclosure. Dr. Bivin and others suspected that while Mike III would probably not live long enough to see a new enclosure, future mascots would certainly benefit from an improved, more natural habitat.

Mike III served as LSU's mascot for eighteen years. During his lifetime LSU won the national championship in football (with a 7–0 win over Clemson) and three SEC championships (in 1958, 1961, 1970); the football team

"Bengal Tiger"

The original of this etching of Mike III, produced for the Alumni Association, hangs in the Kent Anderson Room at the Lod Cook Alumni Center on the LSU campus.

*Etching by Glenn Gore, 1973*

played thirteen bowl games, winning eight of them, and compiled a 142-50-7 record overall. Mike III died of pneumonia on Thursday, August 12, 1976, after the only losing season (5-6-0) of his lifetime. Dr. Bivin helped a local taxidermist remove the pelt. The body of the mascot was cremated, and the pelt was preserved and retained by the taxidermist. Contrary to what many people believe, the tiger on display for many years at a local restaurant in Baton Rouge is not Mike III. That tiger had been shot in the wild by a local hunter and donated to the School of Veterinary Medicine. After some of the veterinary faculty objected to the school having a stuffed animal which had been shot, the school donated the mount to the restaurant.

## MIKE III'S STUDENT CARETAKERS

1958–59: Bill Levenson

1959–61: Douglas Davidson

1961–63: Alvin Meyer Jr.

1963–65: Paul Marks Jr.

1965–68: Joel Samuels

1968–72: Robert Lank Jr.

1972: Philip B. Aman

1972–76: Randy Kilgore

1976: Sonny Corley

# MIKE IV, 1976-1990

Mike IV was born at Busch Gardens in Tampa, Florida, on May 15, 1974. He was abandoned shortly after birth because his mother had health problems, and so he had to be hand raised. He was originally named Jerry. It was hoped that with all of his contact with people, he would be a tame tiger. However, that proved not to be the case. Thanks to a lot of work by the Tiger Booster Club and Jack Gilmore, Mike IV was donated to LSU on August 27, 1976, by August A. Busch III of Busch Gardens. After receiving a clean bill of health from Dr. Earl Schobert, veterinarian for Busch Gardens, the two-year-old, 450-pound tiger arrived at LSU on August 29, 1976.

Five years after his arrival, Mike spent the summer of 1981 at the Little Rock Zoo while

Mike's temporary home at the Little Rock Zoo while his cage in Baton Rouge was being expanded, September 1981.

*Baton Rouge* Advocate

his enclosure was being expanded from four hundred to eleven hundred square feet. The expansion was completed at a cost of about $180,000. The new enclosure was actually supposed to be three times larger and was

Delta Delta Delta fund-raising rally.
*Mark Rayner*

originally expected to cost about $30,000. However, construction cost overruns necessitated scaling down the size of the expansion. It was unfortunate that costs somehow increased so much from the time the first bids were received to the time the job was finished. Both Mike IV and Mike V could have benefited greatly from a larger enclosure. The small size of the enclosure required keeping at least half of the flooring cement. This was very hard on the tigers' feet.

Money for the expansion was raised from many sources. The LSU Student Government Association established the Friends of Mike committee, students attending LSU full time during the summer and fall of 1980 were assessed two dollars each at registration, the Athletic Department contributed, and LSU fans gave generously.

The expansion of Mike's cage was finally done in 1981.
*Gumbo*

Mike IV's expanded home.
*Jim Zietz, University Relations*

Mike IV pins back his ears
and gives a warning to someone behind him.

*Mark Rayner*

Mike IV in March 1982.
*Courtesy Dr. Byron Garrity*

When the expansion was completed and Mike IV returned from Little Rock, it took him some time to adjust to his higher style of living. Mike's keeper at the time, Byron Garrity, says that in his first days in the refurbished surroundings, Mike was very wary of his swimming pool. After about a week, however, he came to love getting in his pool. Mike also didn't know what to make of the grass that had been added to the enclosure. Being raised in captivity, Mike had never seen grass. He would walk around it and put his paw on it but wouldn't walk on it for several days. The grassy area would later be covered over during the reign of Mike V. Tiger urine is very caustic and created dead areas in the grass, quickly turning them to mud. It was feared that so much mud might promote foot infections.

One of the most famous incidents involving the tiger mascots occurred on November

1983 close-up of Mike IV.

28, 1981. At about 1:00 A.M., Dr. Bivin was sound asleep and ill with the flu when he got a call from the LSU police. "Mike's out," they said. "Mike who?" he asked. The police responded, "Mike the tiger. He's out in the middle of North Stadium Drive." How could Mike possibly have escaped? It seems that some pranksters had cut the chain to the outer door and the lock to the inner cage door, releasing the dangerous cat. Once he was convinced that this was not a joke, Dr. Bivin grabbed his rifle and rushed to campus. There he picked up tranquilizers and a dart gun. By the time he arrived on the scene, Mike was wandering around the north end of the Pete Maravich Assembly Center. He ended up in the Bernie Moore Track Stadium. Mike attacked

Mike IV in 1985 gets acquainted with Jim Zietz as he sits close by to photograph the famous tiger.

*Prather Warren, University Relations*

One of the photographs from the session above.

*Jim Zietz, University Relations*

Mike enjoys his pool.
*Jim Zietz, University Relations*

a small tree along the way and appeared to be enjoying himself. Dr. Bivin joined a number of LSU police, including Wayne Ryland, who was the first officer to see the escapee. Police cars were placed at both ends of the stadium to keep Mike inside. They shone their lights toward him. Dr. Bivin bravely went out into the stadium with his tranquilizer pistol in one hand and his rifle in the other. The rifle was to protect himself and others from the tiger. Dr. Bivin managed to get downwind of

Mike. The problem was, he had to be within about forty feet of the tiger to get a clean shot with the tranquilizer pistol. Bivin got as close as he could and got one dart into Mike. The big cat bolted and ran a short way and spun around to see where the dart came from. He spun around again and let out a growl and then a roar. He was mad! Within a few minutes the tranquilizer took effect and his back end became uncoordinated. Dr. Bivin was able to get close enough to get a second dart into

Dr. Bivin visits Mike IV.

*Prather Warren, University Relations*

67

The cheerleaders and student mascot ride through Tiger Stadium with Mike IV on a Saturday night.

*Mark Rayner*

On the road again: Mike IV travels down I-110.

*Mark Rayner*

him. Mike bolted to the north end of the stadium and stood there for a while. Then his back end went down and he was up on only his front feet. He'd get up and then fall down. Finally, he must have decided it was all just too much trouble. He was down and growling but couldn't get up. That's when Dr. Bivin went right up to him and injected him with a third dose. When Mike was completely tranquilized, Dr. Bivin backed his truck up to him and finally coerced the campus police to help him lift Mike into the truck for the short ride back to his cage. Mike awoke the next morning with no ill effects. Shortly after Dr. Bivin returned home, his visiting father found him sitting in the kitchen reflecting on the whole episode. His father said, "Well, doggone, a good night's sleep sure does wonders for you. You sure look better this morning than you did last night." Dr. Bivin had a hard time convincing his father of what had happened during the night!

Throughout his life, Mike IV was a challenge to care for. Occasionally it was Mike who

A close-up view of Mike IV as he focuses on something that has caught his interest. His long, stout whiskers can be easily seen.

*Mark Rayner*

Mike and his student caretaker John D. DeVun, ca. 1985.

*Baton Rouge* Advocate

created a problem, but at other times trouble came from a variety of sources. There was the time when somebody turned a water mocassin loose in Mike's cage and the time Tulane

The regal tiger sits on his perch, ca. 1985.
*Harry M. Cowgill*

students attempted to paint him green. In March 1978, Mike had a root canal performed by Dr. Bivin's dentist, Dr. M. E. Hoover. Mike had broken a canine tooth while trying to get hold of a tire outside his cage. Rather than sticking to the newly available, balanced, commercial diets formulated for zoo cats, Mike loved to bite off pieces of tires and garden hose, chew them up, and swallow them, and

this was not the only time his taste for rubber caused a problem. Twice, in 1977 and again in 1990, he ate at least four feet of hose and required fairly intensive medical care for several days to help him pass all of the pieces. On September 22, 1986, some Texas A&M Aggies threw a Valium-laced hotdog into his cage. Fortunately, it was retrieved before he could eat it. In addition to these episodes, he

Mike IV liked to chew leather and shows his love for football in this photograph.

Mike IV prowls around his home, ca. 1985.

*Harry M. Cowgill*

sometimes had wire cuts, intestinal problems, and sore feet. It is very difficult to provide medical care for a 480-pound man-eating patient with an "attitude."

When asked what closing Mike's cage for the last time would mean to him, John DeVun, Mike IV's caretaker in 1986, replied, "I'll have mixed emotions. First, I can get a fair night's sleep knowing that every time my phone rings late at night it isn't someone telling me the

Visitors gather around Mike's trailer at a School of Veterinary Medicine open house.

*Jim Zietz, University Relations*

tiger has gotten out. It has been something that crosses my mind every time the phone rings." But regretfully, he said, "I'll be sad to be ending something I'll likely never be able to do again. . . . I will be losing a friend."

Mike IV was quite a local traveler. Among other trips, he participated in Mardi Gras parades in Thibodaux, Baton Rouge, and New Orleans. He accompanied LSU to the Sugar Bowl on January 1, 1985, where LSU played Nebraska. Unfortunately Mike's presence was not enough to put the Tigers over the top, and LSU was defeated by Nebraska, 28–10. In

The tiger mascot shows off his pregame antics and his skill with a bow.

*Jim Zietz, University Relations*

addition to his travels, Mike IV had a short but illustrious career as an actor, playing a tiger of course, in the movie *Everybody's All-American,* with costars Dennis Quaid and Jessica Lange. Although the movie was not a box-office smash, it was a good love story involving an LSU football star, and Mike appeared in many scenes. Jeff Larisey, Mike's caretaker at the time, even managed to get some screen-time by dressing up as a cheerleader and accompanying Mike onto the field.

One bizarre event in the life of Mike IV occurred in April 1988. The incident involved Moacyr Cezar, a disgruntled Brazilian who had come to Baton Rouge hoping to secure a job with the Athletic Department. Cezar took the keys from Jeff Larisey and locked himself in the outer portion of the tiger enclosure. The man claimed to have a gun and a bomb and threatened either to shoot or release Mike or explode the bomb. As campus and city police surrounded the tiger enclosure, he continued making threats for five hours. He finally surrendered after about two thousand students gathered around and started chanting, "Eat 'em up, Tigers, eat 'em up!" The man was afraid Mike might be turned loose on him. It turned out that his "gun" was a water pistol and his "bomb" was a sack of books. He was arrested and later returned to Brazil.

Prather Warren, University Relations

Mike IV stands ready for action as he watches something or someone outside of his enclosure. His ears are often pinned back in photographs, an indication of his "all business" personality.

It was during the reign of Mike IV that a car tire was hung in the enclosure. Don Harris reports that one day while Mike was playing with his tire, some LSU football players came by to watch. Inquiring about Mike's strength, they were told that without tying the end of a rope to the enclosure bars, there was no way to keep Mike from running off with the tire. Of course this brought forth challenges from the athletes. Harris locked Mike back in his tiger house, untied the tire from the bars, and had four or five linemen standing outside the bars hold onto the rope. When Harris released Mike from the tiger house, the mascot immediately came and took hold of the tire. The athletes pulled as hard as they could and were about to declare victory in the tug-of-war

when Mike gave a couple of pulls and piled all of the men into the bars. As the players left, they asked if Harris could get Mike into the lineup for the next game, but Harris reminded them that eating the competition was against NCAA rules. Six foot nine, 295-pound LSU defensive end Leonard Marshall, who later played for the New York Giants, had a similar tug-of-war demonstration of Mike IV's strength. This time the rope was looped through the top of the enclosure with Mike and the tire on one end and Marshall on the other. According to eyewitness accounts, Mike pulled down on the tire with such force that Marshall, who was pulling on his end, trying to lift the tire away from Mike, was himself lifted into the air! The other players who were watching were amazed at Mike's incredible strength. Unless one has seen it for oneself, it is difficult to imagine a full-grown tiger's strength.

While Mike IV was normally a very aggressive tiger, he did seem to have a special relationship with at least one of his student caretakers. Jeff Larisey recalls that Mike enjoyed having the bridge of his nose scratched and would rest it between the bars of the fencing for Larisey to rub. Larisey also had a way of getting Mike to act up simply by winking at him. He would wait until the opposing football players were huddled around Mike's trailer on the field and then he would wink at Mike, and the big cat would lunge at the players, scaring them half to death. He could also get Mike excited just by jiggling his keys as he approached the tiger enclosure. The former veterinary student-turned-physician says that caring for Mike and having a close bond with him was and still is a great source of pride.

Mike IV reigned for fourteen years at LSU and retired to the Baton Rouge Zoo in April 1990. Mike had developed a neurologic problem that resulted in mild lameness. In addition, he was getting along in years and was beginning to slow down. It became evident to

Mike snarls into the camera. It was unusual for a photograph to be taken as close as this one because of Mike IV's aggression toward people.

*Prather Warren, University Relations*

Visible in this close-up of Mike IV is his much smaller upper right canine tooth.

*Jim Zietz, University Relations*

Dr. Bivin that Mike IV needed less excitement in his life. The Baton Rouge Zoo graciously offered to take in the aging mascot. There he lived until his condition worsened and he became severely disabled. Mike IV was put to sleep on March 3, 1995. His life span of twenty years, nine months, and eighteen days is considered extremely long for a captive tiger. It is one of the longest on record and the longest of any of the LSU mascots to date. The normal life span of a Bengal tiger is about eight to twelve years in the wild or around fourteen to eighteen years in captivity. After his death it was discovered that in addition to his neural problem, Mike had pneumonia and cancer of the thyroid. The cancer had spread into his chest and to his liver. That finding confirmed that putting Mike IV to sleep had been the most humane option. Mike IV was cremated, and his cremains, along with those of Mike V, are in the Jack and Priscilla Andonie Museum on the LSU campus. When James H. Wharton, chancellor of LSU from 1981 to 1988, was asked about the significance of Mike to LSU, he eloquently stated, "Mike is LSU."

## MIKE IV'S STUDENT CARETAKERS

1976–78: Sonny Corley

1978–80: Sonny Corley & Donald J. Harris Jr.

1980–82: W. Byron Garrity Jr.

1983–84: John R. Allender

1985–86: John D. DeVun

1987–88: Jeff Larisey

1989–90: Jeffrey Perret

Outgoing Mike IV (*left*) and incoming Mike V get acquainted before the elder tiger retired in 1990.

*Harry M. Cowgill*

Mike V

*C. C. Lockwood*

# MIKE V, 1990-2007

Few people know it, but the title "Mike V" was almost taken by a tiger other than the actual Mike V. In the fall of 1989, it became evident that due to declining health, Mike IV should be retired. A new tiger was needed to take his place. George Felton, director of the Baton Rouge Zoo, found a two-and-a-half-week-old male cub at the Wild Wilderness Safari in Arkansas. The cub had been orphaned when his mother died suddenly. Dr. Bivin acquired the tiny cub and brought him to LSU. Because of his young age, the cub was cared for around the clock. However, within a few weeks, it was determined that the cub was completely blind and would never see. He had been born with cataracts. There was nothing that could be done for him. Dr. Bivin knew how difficult the cub's life would be were he to live, so the decision was made to put him to sleep humanely.

Fran Lupp plays with four-and-a-half-month-old Mike V and a toy tiger.
*Baton Rouge* Advocate

81

Mike V's introduction to the
LSU community was at the
LSU-Alabama basketball
game in February 1990.

*Patrick Dennis, Baton Rouge*
Advocate

82

Shortly afterward, the perfect tiger was located. Born October 19, 1989, Mike V was given to LSU by Dr. Thomas and Caroline Atchison of the Animal House Zoological Park in Moulton, Alabama, on February 9, 1990. Charles J. Becker of the Tammany Tigers, an LSU booster group, put Dr. Bivin in touch with the Atchisons. Dr. Bivin traveled to Alabama to examine the four-month-old tiger cub and bring him back if he appeared suitable. The cub exceeded all of Bivin's expectations. Mike V was introduced to LSU fans at the LSU-Alabama basketball game in February 1990, formally "donated" by the Tammany Tigers. He was moved into his cage on April 30 of that year and thus began his reign as Mike V. One of three cubs in his litter, Mike was originally named "Stevie." Reportedly, his sister appeared in a movie about Mother Teresa, and his brother was sent to the Errol Flynn ranch in Aspen, Colorado, with plans to place him on display in a casino. Tom II, a brother of Mike's from a later litter, served as the proud mascot of the University of Memphis until his death in 2008.

Mike V was hand raised. He has been the easiest of the tigers to handle to date.

*Jim Zietz, University Relations*

Chancellor William "Bud" Davis, William Jenkins (then dean of LSU's School of Veterinary Medicine), Dr. Bivin, and William Coleman (then Vice Chancellor for Research) enjoy a day with the cub at the School of Veterinary Medicine.

*Harry M. Cowgill*

"Nobody touch my hat!":
Mike V makes his first "kill"
in the shrubbery on a visit to
the LSU School of Veterinary
Medicine.

*Pat Edwards*

Mike V made his Tiger Stadium debut as the football team started its 97th season in the fall of 1990.

*Baton Rouge* Advocate

Mike V had a calmer, friendlier disposition than most tigers, and so he was relatively easy to care for. This was in large part because he came to LSU at such a young age and was hand raised by loving caretakers. When he was not yet fully grown but was large enough to stand up and grasp people by the back of the neck with his jaws or dunk them under in his swimming pool, he would do so playfully. But when his weight topped 250 pounds, the decision was made to no longer allow people

Lucas LeBoeuf and Harry Cowgill watch Mike as he swims in the pool within his enclosure.

*Jim Zietz, University Relations*

85

*Harry M. Cowgill*

Mike licks his mouth clean
after enjoying a good snack.

*C. C. Lockwood*

photographer. When he came back around for another "attack," Norris grabbed the photographer, threw him out of the enclosure, pushed Mike firmly on the nose, and got himself out before Mike decided to get aggressive. While it is unlikely that Mike would really have attacked with the intent to injure, one can't take chances with a 250-pound tiger. Norris's partner, Shelly Phillips, was the first woman to serve as a tiger caretaker. Caretakers have usually been male because of the physical requirements of the job. Phillips recalls the special opportunity she and Norris had to work with Mike V as a cub. As Mike aged through adulthood, Phillips was reluctant to visit him because she so enjoyed the contact with him as a cub and wanted to remember him that way.

into his enclosure with him. At that weight, Mike might accidentally hurt someone. And because he was a tiger and not a domestic animal, a day would probably come when his wild instincts would emerge and he might attack someone.

Rollie Norris was the last student caretaker to have contact with Mike with no bars between them. One day Norris took a photographer into Mike's enclosure. They thought Mike was safely locked on the other side of a gate. Much to their surprise, however, the gate was open! Mike came through the gate and ran right over the top of the terrified

An empty keg was a popular toy of Mike's. Its use was discontinued during an alcohol awareness campaign on campus.

*Jan Leonard*

Mike V's first road trip was to the Superdome in December 1991 for a basketball game against Texas (which, with the help of Shaquille O'Neal, the Tigers won, 84–83). Apparently Mike was not very impressed with his trailer. He spent much of the return trip ripping the wire mesh off the back of it. Rollie Norris recalls that as a student, Shaquille O'Neal would often visit Mike at his cage. However, when given the opportunity to come inside for a closer look, O'Neal always declined. It seems he was content to observe Mike from well outside the enclosure.

Mike V usually cooperated when it was time to load him into his trailer. In this regard, he was easier to work with than his predecessors. To ensure Mike's well-being, however, off-campus travel was restricted. Whenever Mike V left campus, he was escorted by a uniformed LSU police officer. Even the LSU police officers who were not graduates of LSU considered it an honor to serve as Mike's escort. This is one of the many important behind-the-scenes aspects of caring for a tiger mascot. Mike's veterinarians have always greatly appreciated the tremendous support provided by the LSU Police Department.

Like Mike IV before him, Mike V presented his caretakers with a number of challenges. For example, in September 1996, Mike developed an overgrown and ingrown claw. As a result, he became lame and was completely

Dr. Baker trains Nelson Lewis, one of the veterinary student tiger caretakers, to use the sedative dart gun in case of an emergency.

*Harry Cowgill*

Dr. Jerry Ford in 2001 with his purple and white 1959 Chevrolet El Camino. It was during his first visit to campus in 1959 that Jerry became captivated by Mike III and LSU.

*Courtesy Jerry Ford*

unwilling for his new veterinarian, Dr. David Baker, to examine his foot. Baker had to heavily sedate Mike in order to examine and treat his paw. In April 1997, Mike somehow broke his upper right canine tooth, exposing the pulp cavity. A root canal was performed on May 13 by Dr. Ben Colmery, a veterinary dentist from Michigan. Because a tiger's canine tooth is so long, special equipment is needed to extract the entire root. Dr. Colmery had the needed equipment and had performed the procedure on several tigers. While Mike lay anesthetized on the operating table, it was Dr. Baker who did the pacing as he waited anxiously for the surgery to end. With that

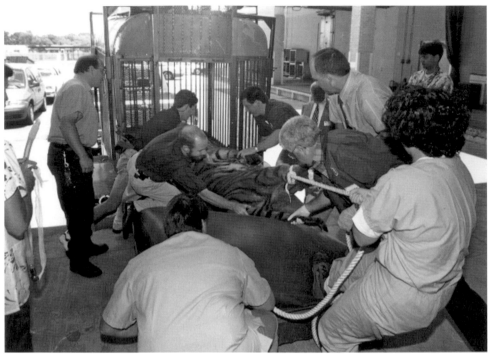

The first time Mike was taken for a root canal was on May 13, 1997.
*Harry M. Cowgill*

Dr. Alfred Stevens performs a second root canal on Mike on July 13, 2000.
*Harry M. Cowgill*

Mike enjoys an oxtail once a week, which helps keep his teeth clean.

*C. C. Lockwood*

procedure, Mike V became the third LSU tiger to require a root canal. Dental problems are common in tigers and are, indirectly, the leading cause of their death in the wild. As tigers age, their teeth become more brittle and are easily damaged or broken. In addition to Mike's standard daily ration of five to ten pounds of a commercially prepared diet of meat, fish, soy, vegetables, vitamins, and minerals, he was given an oxtail once per week. This practice continues today. The oxtail is an important part of Mike's dental health because it helps keep his teeth clean and maintain his jaw strength.

Providing Mike V with adequate environmental enrichment was another challenge.

Abnormal behaviors could result if Mike became too bored in his small enclosure. His caretakers frequently devised new ways to keep him stimulated. For example, they would

This grassy area would later be covered over because tiger urine is very caustic and created dead areas in the grass, quickly turning them to mud.

*Harry M. Cowgill*

Mike sits in the shade and out of the heat as much as possible.

*Harry M. Cowgill*

hide his food in different places, construct artificial prey for him to tear apart, and place unusual scents in his enclosure. Matthew Wheelock recalls purchasing a kiddie pool for Mike. The plan was to get him used to the pool and then add fish. Surely Mike would love to watch the fish swim. Unfortunately, the plan broke down before any fish were added. It seemed Mike didn't need the fish. He was happy just to destroy the pool! Mike's caretakers tried pools of at least four different colors in hopes of finding one that he wouldn't want to destroy. They never found a suitable pool, so the plan was abandoned. The experiment was not a total failure, however, because Mike certainly was entertained in the process!

On July 13, 2000, with the assistance of Dr. Gordon Pirie of the Baton Rouge Zoo, Dr.

Mike cools off by panting after playing with a toy on a hot day.

*Jim Zietz, University Relations*

Baker removed a tumor from Mike's abdominal wall. Mike is visually examined twice daily, and Baker had noticed the enlargement while observing Mike a few days earlier. An ultrasound-guided biopsy confirmed that it was a tumor. While Drs. Baker and Pirie were removing the tumor, Dr. Kem Singletary and Dr. Alfred Stevens, a local practitioner with special expertise in veterinary dentistry, performed dental repairs. Stevens had assisted with Mike's root canal in 1997 and now was equipped to do the dental work himself. The dental procedure was necessary because the unwilling patient had damaged a tooth during the ultrasound examination. After surgery, Mike V remained overnight at the School of Veterinary Medicine. Prior to returning him to his cage the next day, Matthew Wheelock and Kirk Maurer, Mike's veterinary student caretakers, drained his five-foot-deep pool. It was feared that if Mike was still affected at all by the anesthetics, he might fall into his pool and drown.

In November 2001, Mike developed a temporary thyroid problem, which resulted in considerable weight loss and hormonal changes. Fortunately, however, the problem passed, and Mike returned to his normal, healthy condition. As Mike aged, it was anticipated that medical problems would become more common. In that regard he was certainly like the rest of us. However, one can imagine the difficulty in providing excellent medical care for an aging animal that prefers not to be handled by his doctor. When Mike V was younger, most minor medical procedures were performed without the use of sedatives or anesthetics. But there was some risk in even temporarily confining Mike in his metal "squeeze chute" while a physical examination was performed or blood samples were collected. So as Mike V aged, Dr. Baker began sedating him when medical procedures were necessary.

By September 1997, the trailer used for forty years—since Mike II—to transport LSU's mascot had worn out. A new trailer was clearly needed to move Mike V safely. A beautiful

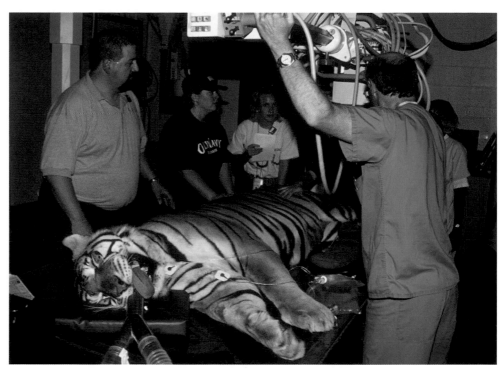

While Mike is anesthetized, technicians at the School of Veterinary Medicine prepare to take x-rays of his hip.

*Harry M. Cowgill*

Dr. David Baker (*right*), assisted by Dr. Gordon Pirie of the Baton Rouge Zoo, removes a tumor from Mike's abdominal wall.

*Harry M. Cowgill*

The tiger trailer received a fresh coat of paint from Troy LeBlanc, seen here standing with the trailer.

*Phillip Cancilleri*

This inventive mailbox, an exact replica of the trailer that carries Mike, belongs to Harold Doyle Jr. of Slidell.

new trailer was graciously donated to LSU by Doug Guidroz and Rick Vallet, owners of Central Hitch and Equipment in Baton Rouge. The expert trailer manufacturers had already constructed a number of high-quality trailers for the School of Veterinary Medicine. Dr. Baker therefore felt confident that the sturdy new tiger taxi would serve Mike V well into the future. A contest was held to allow the public to suggest the color scheme for the new trailer. Some wild designs were submitted. The winning design was drawn by Al Carter, and the new trailer was painted beautiful LSU gold with purple lettering. The bars making up the cage portion of the trailer were painted white in order to reflect and reduce heat on sunny days. Many fans wanted the bars painted black for increased visibility of the tiger, but that could result in Mike overheating on hot days. Thanks to a lot of hard work by the crew of Central Hitch and Equipment over the Labor Day weekend, the new trailer was ready in time for the home opener against the University of Texas–El Paso on September 6, 1997.

A pensive Mike.

*Jim Zietz, University Relations*

A poster showing all of the LSU tigers through the years, produced by the Baton Rouge *Advocate* for the 1996 football season.

*Courtesy Clay Stewart*

One need only imagine the dangers of being stranded with a broken-down trailer and a nearly 400-pound tiger to appreciate the importance of a sturdy trailer for the safety of Mike and his caretakers.

On January 1, 2002, Mike V once again ventured to the Superdome in New Orleans, this time to support the football team in its game against the University of Illinois in the Nokia Sugar Bowl. Unusually cold temperatures had been predicted for the week, and for once the

forecasters turned out to be right. To protect Mike from the cold, his caretakers bedded his trailer deeply with straw and secured it with a custom-made cover. The back was closed up with plywood sheets modified by Dr. Baker's eleven-year-old son, Martin. Dr. Baker even took a test ride in the trailer to make sure there were no chilling drafts coming in. Mike was accompanied by Dr. Baker and his caretakers Matthew Wheelock and Kirk Maurer, along with three guests. In addition, the LSU police sent along an officer in a squad car as an escort. Shortly after the group left Baton Rouge, freezing rain began to fall. Mike stayed for the first half of what was turning into a very long game. Not wanting to risk being involved in an accident if the roads froze, the tiger team elected to leave ahead of the crowd, which proved to be a wise decision. It snowed nearly all the way back to LSU. Mike reached the campus just as the game was ending in a 48–34 victory for the Tigers. He had enjoyed a long and eventful day, but rather than going directly into his house to rest, he first investigated the soft, cold, white powder that had coated his entire enclosure. This was probably Mike's first experience with snow. He cautiously smelled it, tasted it, pawed at it, and slipped on it. After several minutes of investigating this new substance, he lost interest and retired to his warm house for a good night's sleep.

By 2000 it became evident that to continue housing a live tiger on the LSU campus, a new enclosure was required so that Mike V and all future Mikes could enjoy a more healthful environment. University officials had discussed the need for a new home for Mike for several years. But now, the deteriorating condition of the original enclosure, coupled with Mike's chronic foot problems associated with prolonged housing on concrete and other man-made surfaces, required action. A larger, more environmentally enriched facility with water, trees, shrubs, grass, and other natural substrates was envisioned. The Tiger Athletic Foundation took on the monumental project. A fund-raising committee, led by Mrs. De-Laine Emmert and Mr. Bill Hulsey, worked with the Tiger Athletic Foundation to raise the $3.2 million needed for construction and endowment. The Tiger Athletic Foundation's "Party for an Animal" kicked off the fund-raising drive on May 11, 2002, at the home of head football coach Nick Saban. The response from the LSU community was tremendous.

Mike makes a purple paw-print for the limited edition of *Mike the Tiger: The Roar of LSU* in 2003. The nontoxic purple ink was quite tasty to Mike, and he got it all over himself.

*Kevin Bankston*

George Rodrigue painting *Mike the Tiger 2003*.

*Jacques Rodrigue*

This fresco was removed from the original night house and preserved as a historical artifact.

*Berkman Manuel of Gibbs Construction*

Construction of Mike's new habitat, 2003.

*Berkman Manuel of Gibbs Construction*

Ribbon-cutting ceremony, August 2005. *From left:* Larry Gibbs of Gibbs Construction, student body president Michelle Gieg, Miss LSU-USA Katherine Ellard, David Baker, Tiger Athletic Foundation board member H. F. Anderson, Chancellor Sean O'Keefe, DeLaine Emmert with student mascot, Bill Hulsey (co-chair with DeLaine Emmert of the fundraising effort), Athletic Director Skip Bertman, LSU System President William L. Jenkins, student government representative Jason Dorè, architect Ace Torre, and Ron Richard of the Tiger Athletic Foundation.

*LSU Chancellor's Office, Photo Archive*

In 2003, local artist and avid LSU fan George Rodrigue, famous for his "Blue Dog" paintings, contributed his prodigious talents to the cause. A group of concerned LSU students, including the artist's son Jacques, had approached Mr. Rodrigue about creating a Blue Dog–themed painting to help raise money for Mike's new habitat. Instead, the artist painted a swamp scene of Mike the Tiger in a cypress tree! It was an immediate hit. Print sales raised more than $1 million toward a new home for Mike.

The 13,000-square-foot enclosure was

Visitors can see above and below the water line of Mike's new pool.

*Wendy Day*

Mike enjoys his new stream.
*Bobbie Grand*

designed by Ace Torre, an LSU alumnus who had created zoo animal exhibits all over the country. The design incorporated an Italianate campanile as an exhibit backdrop as well as an LSU-style colonnade façade for viewing and restraint. The habitat included a waterfall, stream, and pool, and allowed Mike to get among the shrubbery and out of the weather at all times of the year. Prior to demolition of the original enclosure, Dr. Baker asked that the frescoes be removed from the night house and preserved as historical artifacts by the Athletic Department.

Mike was transferred to his temporary home at BREC's Baton Rouge Zoo on November 23, 2004. While there, he was lovingly cared for by zookeeper Holly Taylor. Mike returned to LSU and his new, permanent home

Mike in his spacious new habitat.
*Dawn Forste*

on August 26, 2005, just three days before Hurricane Katrina slammed the Gulf Coast. Mike rode out the hurricane in the safety of his new night house. For several days he watched with great interest as helicopters ferried people to the nearby Pete Maravich Assembly Center, where a medical triage unit had been established. After things settled back down, and once he assured himself that he was the only tiger around, Mike adapted quickly to his new enclosure. As hoped, the larger,

environmentally enriched space was much more interesting for Mike, providing wholesome surroundings for him and for many Mikes to come.

The reign of Mike V was punctuated with a highly successful collegiate sports program: 29 national championships in six sports. Most notably, the women's track-and-field teams won an amazing 19 national championships between indoor and outdoor venues. During the same period, the men's track-and-field teams clinched four national championships, and the baseball team won five national championships. One of the most exciting victories during the reign of Mike V was LSU's 31–14 defeat of Oklahoma on January 4, 2004, to win the BCS National Championship for the 2003 football season. It was LSU's second national championship in football in the school's history.

While there are countless stories about the impact LSU's live tigers have made on people, two incidents concerning Mike V in particular stand out. The first happened on October 19, 1997, Mike V's eighth birthday. Dr. Baker

These football fans show their love for Mike and Tiger football.

*C. C. Lockwood*

Mike stays in his new night house during Hurricane Katrina.

*Wendy Day*

arrived at Mike's enclosure to find a young girl in an LSU cheerleader's costume tying a birthday card to the fence of Mike's enclosure. When Dr. Baker asked her about it, she told him that she and Mike V shared the same birthday. She too was eight years old. She said that every year her grandmother brought her to Mike's house so she could leave him a birthday card and wish him well. Dr. Baker was so touched by her devotion to Mike that he took a picture of the two of them together, separated only by the fence. No doubt the little girl will cherish that photograph. She may even have

attended LSU as a student, and she will very likely go through her adulthood sensitive to the endangered wildlife with which we share this planet. The second story involves a friend of Dr. Baker's whose mother was dying. As a small token of his appreciation for all she had done for him, the friend wrote down sixty acts his mother had performed for which he was very thankful. He had these professionally inscribed by a calligrapher, matted, and framed, and he presented the gift to his mother, who was then in the hospital. Toward the top of the list was written, "Thank you for taking me

Mike tries out his new pool.
*Wendy Day*

to see Mike the tiger." The Sunday afternoon visits to see Mike that his mother had treated him to as a young boy had in some small way strengthened the special bond between them.

In the spring of 2007, Mike's caretakers observed that he was contending with a number of age-related health issues. For example, he appeared to have developed sensitivity in his lower incisors, which had worn considerably over the course of his long life. This resulted in a decreased appetite and contributed to a loss of nearly seventy pounds of body weight. It was determined that Mike should be given a thorough examination, even though anesthesia is risky in elderly animals. On May 15, Mike was observed having trouble breathing. He was fasted overnight in preparation for anesthesia the following morning. After receiving his medication, he was taken to the School of Veterinary Medicine, where it was determined that Mike had a considerable amount of fluid on his lungs. The source could not be located, but the fluid was removed nonetheless. Unfortunately, Mike's aged kidneys, unable to handle the reduced blood flow that occurs under anesthesia, failed. All steps, including renal dialysis (a historic first in tiger medicine), were taken to pull Mike through, but his kidneys simply would not resume proper function. At 2:23 A.M. on May 18, 2007, forty-two hours after being anesthetized, Mike died.

Veterinary students David Schur and Verna

Dr. Baker presents plaques to Matthew Wheelock (*left*) and Kirk Maurer in May 2002, thanking them for caring for Mike V.

*Courtesy LSU Athletic Department*

The changing of the guard: Steve Eastman and Leath Harper (*back*) take over the role of Mike's caretakers from David Webre and Shane Parker (*front*) in the spring of 1998.

Serra helped Dr. Baker place Mike's body in a secure location until it could be cremated later that day. It was a particularly hard day for the LSU community to lose Mike V because it was also graduation day. Many new graduates, their families, and their friends visited Mike's enclosure expecting to see him lounging in the shade but instead found a floral wreath signifying his passing. The Athletic Department set up a website so that Mike's admirers could send in their condolences. Nearly 750 messages were received. Then-governor Kathleen Blanco expressed the feelings of many when she said, "Mike V served LSU as more than a mascot. He was an epic symbol that represented the unique spirit of our state's flagship university."

## CONDOLENCES FOLLOWING THE DEATH OF MIKE V

"How well I remember the day all those years ago at the Assembly Center when they trotted out the little cub that would grow to be Mike the Tiger. Rest well, old friend."

—Scotty Drake, Baton Rouge, LA

"You have reigned supreme . . . these are big paws to fill!!!!"

—Karen Gerarve, Harahan, LA

"We will love you and remember you always!"

—Rita Harris, Shreveport, LA

"Ever since I first stepped onto campus, you have been a great part of my experience at LSU . . . Mike V you are Forever LSU."

—Michael Whitman, Lake Charles, LA

"I was married in front of Mike's cage, so he was the first one there for the ceremony."

—Jami-Lynn Graham, Baton Rouge, LA

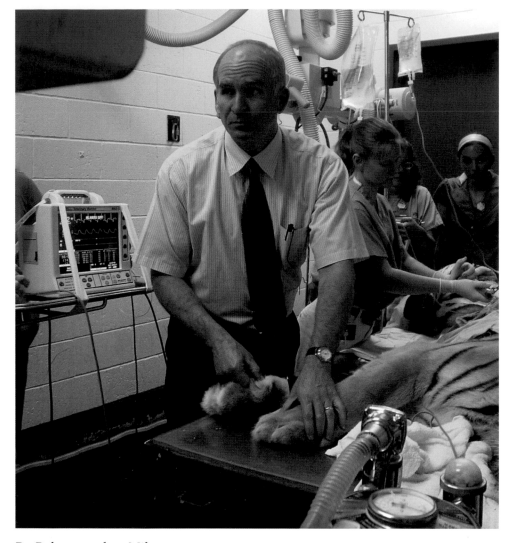

Dr. Baker attends to Mike while Dr. Loretta Bubenik removes fluid from Mike's chest cavity.

*Ginger Guttner*

Cartoon by David Norwood.

*Reprinted by permission of* The Advocate

"Mike was an awesome sight to behold. . . . He was feared all over the SEC and the Nation. But he was loved by child and adult alike within the LSU Nation."

—Joseph Matta, Covington, LA

"My son learned to spell T-I-G-E-R-S before he could spell his own name thanks to Mike. What great memories (and stern looks from the wife) that has given us!"

—Rodney Blackwell, Little Rock, AR

"Mike V represented all of what we want and hope Louisiana State University is and gives to its students, faculty, and citizens of Louisiana: beauty, strength, and pride."

—Anonymous

## MIKE V'S STUDENT CARETAKERS

1990: Jeffrey Perret

1990–92: Rollie Norris and Shelly Phillips

1992–94: Jeffery Artall and Mark Gentry

1994–96: Lance Hidalgo and Randolph Hayes

1996–98: L. Shane Parker and David B. Webre

1998–2000: Leath Harper Jr. and Stephen Eastman

2000–02: Matthew Wheelock and Kirk Maurer

2002–04: Kevin Bankston and Blake Tunnard

2004–06: Nelson Lewis and Timothy "Toby" Wallis

2006–07: Wendy Day and Wesley Lee

Memorials for Mike V.

*David G. Baker*

Student caretakers Kevin Bankston and Blake Tunnard.

*Phillip Cancilleri*

Wendy Day and Wesley Lee, Mike V's last caretakers and Mike VI's first caretakers.

*Sandy Oubre*

A stately Mike VI.

*Christine Russell*

# MIKE VI, 2007-PRESENT

Having Mike the Tiger puts LSU in a relatively small community of universities with live animal mascots. In fact, there are only about forty colleges and universities with live mascots. The majority of these are dogs, which are clearly more easily cared for and handled than a tiger. Within the SEC, most of the people who care for their university's mascot know or are at least familiar with their counterparts at other schools. Dr. Baker occasionally communicates with persons at other universities within the SEC regarding animal welfare and other issues pertaining to their mascots. In some cases, close, "virtual" relationships have even formed between the mascots. For example, when Mike V had one of his root canal procedures, Uga V, the bulldog

mascot of the University of Georgia, sent him a get-well card. Now that's unusual; a dog wishing a cat well! And when Mike V died, Tusk II, the razorback mascot from the University of Arkansas, sent a bouquet of black

This cartoon by David Norwood that appeared in the Baton Rouge *Advocate* comments on protests over LSU's plan to find a new tiger after Mike V's death.

*Reprinted by permission of* The Advocate

Roscoe at age five weeks.
*Donna Cotner*

a colleague with the U.S. Department of Agriculture. Mike VI would have to be a confident, healthy, well-proportioned, and beautiful male Bengal or Bengal-cross tiger. Contact with the facility owner, Rob Craig, confirmed that it had what LSU was looking for.

So, on June 25, 2007, Dr. Baker, accompanied by Dr. Gordon Pirie of the Baton Rouge Zoo, flew to Indiana to have a look. There they were introduced to Roscoe, a beautiful, two-year-old Bengal-Siberian cross. Compared to Mike V, who was a Bengal-Indochinese cross, Roscoe had a longer muzzle; more white on his face and undersides; a larger ruff, which is smaller but somewhat similar to a lion's mane; and more double stripes, which make for a tiger of truly stunning appearance. Born July 23, 2005, Roscoe was the product of a breeding that occurred when his father, Tigger, an enormous Siberian tiger weighing perhaps 700 to 800 pounds, tore down his enclosure fence and bred two female tigers in the adjacent pen. Roscoe's mother, Kiara, was a graceful, Bengal-cross tiger with striking markings. Drs. Baker and Pirie were impressed with much of what they saw at Great Cats of Indiana, including the overall excellent condition of the seventy carnivores residing there, Tigger's massive size, and the extensive care shown to each animal by the Great Cats crew. It didn't take Dr. Baker long to decide that Roscoe belonged at LSU.

roses. That in itself was somewhat ironic because if given the opportunity, Mike V might have eaten that pig!

The search for Mike V's replacement began the day he died. While a tiger could be obtained from a zoo or a breeder, the preferred source was a licensed rescue facility. Use of the Internet, a communication medium not available during the searches for previous tigers, allowed Dr. Baker to quickly obtain information about many available tigers without having to actually visit all of them. A suitable source was found in Great Cats of Indiana, a privately run rescue facility near Idaville, Indiana. Dr. Baker learned about the facility from

Roscoe in his first home in Indiana. He has more double stripes on his body than did any previous LSU tiger.

*Rob Craig*

Before he could cross state lines, Roscoe needed a physical examination and health certificate from a veterinarian licensed in the state of Indiana. Fortunately, LSU alumna and Dr. Baker's former graduate student Dr. Robin Crisler-Roberts met all the necessary qualifications. Crisler-Roberts was excited and proud to provide this service for her alma mater. She examined Roscoe on August 18, 2007, and found him to be in excellent health. He was vaccinated in preparation for the trip.

Back in Baton Rouge, planning began to bring Roscoe to LSU. A transport crate was constructed by Bobby Wascom of MG Trailer Depot, and an airplane owned by Acadian Ambulance was prepared. Details regarding Roscoe and plans for his transport were withheld from the public so that if something went wrong and he never arrived at LSU, or was later found unsuitable to become Mike VI, the LSU community would not already have formed an attachment to the tiger. While this approach was a source of great frustration to many in the media, the university

Roscoe is loaded into a crate at his old home near Idaville, Indiana, for his trip to Louisiana.

*Rhett Stout*

Roscoe is loaded onto a plane for his flight to Baton Rouge.

*Rhett Stout*

Roscoe arrives at his new home at LSU.

*Rhett Stout*

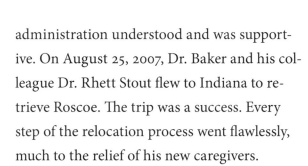

Roscoe spends his first week at LSU in his night house.

*Rhett Stout*

administration understood and was supportive. On August 25, 2007, Dr. Baker and his colleague Dr. Rhett Stout flew to Indiana to retrieve Roscoe. The trip was a success. Every step of the relocation process went flawlessly, much to the relief of his new caregivers.

Roscoe was quarantined and acclimated inside his night house his first week at LSU. At 5:45 P.M. on Friday, August 31, Dr. Baker notified LSU Public Relations that "Mike VI" would be released into his yard the following day at 9:00 A.M. The Public Relations office sent an email message to LSU alumni and other friends, announcing the pending release. Bright and early the next morning, there were over one thousand people waiting to see the new mascot. Dr. Baker spoke with one family from Kentucky who were preparing dinner when the announcement came through. Upon learning of the coming event, they turned off their stove, got in their car, and drove to LSU. Another family from Texas said that upon receiving the notice, they finished their dinner and drove to LSU. Many people considered the tiger's release to be a historic moment they wanted to share with their children.

At exactly 9:00 A.M., Roscoe was released from his night house. The moment he stepped into his yard for the first time, he was no longer Roscoe but was now Mike VI. He was confident but naturally cautious as he explored his new home. He first moved along the perimeter of the habitat, carefully watching the rock formation on the opposite side, until he was convinced that there were no other tigers in the enclosure. He then explored the grassy areas of his yard, and finally, got into his pool. He was very interested in the people gazing at him through protective glass and got as close to them as he could. It is important to keep in mind that until that day, he had never seen a plant, nor had he ever seen more water than was in a bucket. One can only imagine what

was going through his mind as he explored what must have seemed like paradise to him.

The 320-pound tiger was an immediate hit with the LSU faithful who showed up to greet the new mascot. Many were surprised by his large size and his energy level. Photos and videos of the new tiger playing and interacting with visitors through the glass of his enclosure spread quickly over the Internet. Through these images as well as personal visits, the LSU community soon developed an intense love for their new tiger. In a special ceremony held at his enclosure on September 14, 2007, he was officially welcomed as Mike VI by LSU Chancellor Sean O'Keefe.

Upon release from his night house, Mike VI first walks the perimeter of his habitat.
*Ginger Guttner*

Roscoe emerges from his night house and becomes Mike VI.

*Michael A. Westphal*

Developmentally, Mike was roughly equivalent to a ten-year-old boy at the time he came to LSU. Can you imagine how much had changed in his life? He had left his original family for a new one without other tigers, and his surroundings had changed considerably. He had a new daily diet of 20–30 pounds of commercial carnivore food, a weekly oxtail, and an occasional whole chicken or small pig—already dead, of course. With all of these changes in his life, Mike needed companionship, and he found it in his caretakers, with whom he quickly formed strong relationships. Tigers normally live alone in the wild as adults, but they enjoy the companionship of other tigers while they are young. For Mike, humans would have to do. He easily came to

recognize his caretakers. For example, Mike learned the fragrance worn by one of his caretakers, and as soon as he caught the scent of her perfume, he would perk up and look for her. Interestingly, Mike still recognizes and gets excited to see his original student caretakers, long after they have left LSU and become practicing veterinarians.

Having formally assumed the title of Mike VI, the new mascot next had to prepare to participate in the football pregame activities. Wendy Day and Wesley Lee, Mike's veterinary student caretakers, began getting him accustomed to his travel trailer, which now bore his name. Early one morning Mike was loaded into his trailer and driven inside Tiger Stadium, following the same route he would

Mike VI's first day on view.
*Tim Morgan*

Mike VI gets to know his fans.
*Michael A. Westphal*

Wendy Day gives Mike a snack.
*Ginger Guttner*

take on game day. He was very calm throughout the short ride. However, riding around inside an empty stadium is quite different from entering a stadium with thousands of noisy fans. How would he respond to that? The test came on October 6, 2007, when LSU hosted the University of Florida. It had originally been planned to take Mike to the previous week's game against the University of South Carolina, but Dr. Baker had postponed Mike's football debut until a night game, when it would be cooler. It was a beautiful fall evening as Mike VI made his entry into Tiger Stadium. The way leading to the stadium was lined with fans, standing dozens deep. In fact, it was estimated that as many as 40,000 more

Nicholas Cross and Randee Monceaux play with Mike.
*Christine Russell*

Mike on the field for his first game. Dr. Gordon Pirie of the Baton Rouge Zoo is visible on the far left.

*Phillip Cancilleri*

people than usual came to LSU that day just to see Mike VI. Their reactions indicated their love for Mike and the desire that this important tradition live on. Some people were laughing and pointing, others were standing silent with their hands over their mouths, while still others were weeping. As soon as the trailer pulled into Tiger Stadium, Dr. Baker and Dr. Pirie, who were accompanying Mike, turned to each other and agreed that they had never sensed such emotion from the crowd and that it was not something they expected to experience ever again. In honor of the new mascot, LSU defeated Florida 28–24. It was a great start to Mike's career. In fact, ultimately Mike VI would follow in the pawprints of Mike III by seeing LSU defeat Ohio State 38–24 in New Orleans for the 2007 season BCS National

Mike's first football game. Eye—and nose—of the tiger.

*David G. Baker*

Fans crowd on the PMAC ramp as well as around his trailer to see Mike on his first game day.

*Ginger Guttner*

Meeting of the Mikes.

*Scott Soileau—TigerRoar.com*

Championship in his first season as the reigning Mike the Tiger.

Mike VI has a remarkably engaging, playful, and confident personality. He regularly "chuffs" his greetings to those whom he recognizes, especially his caretakers, who do all they can to preserve his excellent disposition. During Mike's first few seasons at LSU, the student mascot tiger was asked not to approach Mike on the football field to elicit the traditional roar prior to the football game. The plan was to wait until Mike matured to resume this tradition. However, by Mike's fourth season the decision was made to discontinue the practice permanently. Dr. Baker has always placed Mike's well-being above concerns related to

Obie O'Brien's yard in Dallas before the 2011 Cotton Bowl (LSU versus Texas A&M University).

*Phillip Cancilleri*

athletic events, and he determined that allowing the student mascot to enter Mike's personal space to elicit a roar was not in Mike's best interests. Most in the LSU community supported this decision.

Ensuring the well-being of the human community is also a priority, and sometimes that causes Mike's fans disappointment. For example, a nearby daycare center asked if Mike could come over and play with the children. Others have similarly asked why no one enters Mike's enclosure to play with him. Still others have asked whether Mike could be turned loose on the football field for photo opportunities. Such requests may stem from the recollection of seeing people play with Mike V when he was a small cub. Mike VI does have a playful and friendly personality like his predecessor. However, tigers are not pets; they are wild animals. In addition, Mike weighs nearly 500 pounds and could easily cause injury even without intending to do so.

Mike playing with Dr. Baker.
*Christine Russell*

Old holding cell of previous night house.

*Berkman Manuel of Gibbs Construction*

Current holding cell in Mike's night house.

*Berkman Manuel of Gibbs Construction*

Some fans have expressed disappointment when Mike does not appear on the field before a football game. Fans should know that Mike is not prodded or forced into his trailer to attend a game. In fact, there is no safe way to do so, and those who care for Mike believe strongly that he should not be forced to go to an athletic event. The night house of the previous enclosure was fitted with a pivoting wall that could be used to force Mike to enter his trailer. The current night house is not fitted with a similar gate.

A fully mature Mike VI.

*Christine Russell*

Mike VI on patrol.

*Christine Russell*

Tiger display at LSU's Museum of Natural History.
*Eddy Perez*

Tiger display at Alex Box Stadium.
*Ginger Guttner*

Since coming to LSU, Mike has grown into a healthy and handsome, fully mature tiger. He is much larger than Mike V, who weighed around 400 pounds at his peak, and he is about the same size as Mike IV, previously LSU's heaviest tiger. He will not get taller or longer, but he will likely fill out a bit. Dr. Baker plans to limit Mike's weight so that he remains active and healthy. Maintaining the long-term health of a tiger is challenging. Fortunately, Mike VI has had few medical issues. Compared to wild tigers, captive tigers are generally very healthy since they are free from nearly all infectious diseases and do not have to capture and kill their food or defend their territory. In addition, Mike benefits from LSU's excellent School of Veterinary Medicine, with its highly qualified veterinarians and the most advanced clinical resources.

In 2011 and 2012, interactive tiger education displays were created with support from a Department of Housing and Urban Development grant. The first display is located in the Louisiana Museum of Natural History on the LSU campus and incorporates the mounted skin of Mike I. The second is located in the new Alex Box baseball stadium. These displays allow thousands of guests per year to learn about Mike and about the conservation of tigers and other endangered species. In this way, Mike the Tiger shares in the university's educational mission.

Being a modern tiger, Mike has entered the age of social media. He has his own Facebook page, and his life events are communicated via Twitter. Video and still photos of Mike abound on the Internet. Because of the availability of electronic communications, Mike VI has perhaps become the best known of all the LSU tiger mascots.

## MIKE VI'S STUDENT CARETAKERS

2007–08: Wendy Day and Wesley Lee

2008–10: Adam Caro and Kelly Folse

2010–12: Nicholas Cross and Randee Monceaux

2012–14: Daniel Cutler and Macy Trosclair

Caretakers Nicholas Cross, Macy Trosclair, Daniel Cutler, and Randee Monceaux.

*Christine Russell*

Mike VI gets up close to his adoring fans.

*Michael A. Westphal*

# More about Mike

It is estimated that Mike receives roughly 100,000 visitors per year. Because he lives in view on the LSU campus, it is natural for people to ask many questions about him. Here are some of the most frequent queries.

### Does Mike "meow" like a cat?

No. Large cats do not "meow" like domestic cats. Tigers make four sounds. A chuff (or prustin) is a happy sound and is used in greeting. The moan reveals minor concern or anxiety. A tiger growls as a warning to other tigers (or to his veterinarian). Finally, a roar is used as an aggressive warning or to locate other tigers in the wild.

### Is Mike ever given a bath?

No. Mike cannot be handled as if he were a pet or domestic animal. Mike grooms himself regularly. Also, Mike spends a lot of time in his swimming pool. In addition to cooling him off on hot days, this helps his body stay clean.

Michael A. Westphal

### Is Mike neutered or declawed?

No. There is no valid medical reason for either of these procedures. Having all of his body parts allows Mike to develop normally and to express normal, species-specific behaviors other than breeding.

### Does Mike get his claws clipped?

No. Mike keeps his claws sharp and at the right length by pulling them on the oak stump placed in his yard. One time, when the stump fell over, Mike V would not use it and one of his claws grew too long and had to be trimmed by Dr. Baker. Since then, Mike's caretakers have always made sure that his oak stump is standing upright.

### What does Mike eat?

Long ago, tigers in captivity were fed only muscle meat. As they aged, this diet often resulted in the development of arthritis. Mike VI eats a balanced, commercially prepared diet made especially for large cats. It is the consistency of hamburger but is made of horsemeat or beef, fish, vitamins, minerals, and vegetables. This diet is supplemented with extra vitamins.

Mike is fed twenty to thirty pounds of food per day. As he ages, he will be fed less to keep him at a healthy weight.

### Is Mike ever fed live animals?

No. It is not necessary to feed Mike live animals. We would not want the prey animals to have to be killed by Mike since they could suffer in the process. Also, it is possible that Mike could be injured in the process of killing an animal. So, for the benefit of Mike and potential prey, he is not fed live animals.

### How does Mike keep his teeth clean?

In the wild, a tiger keeps its teeth relatively clean by chewing on the bones of the animals it has killed. Because Mike doesn't kill animals, he is given an oxtail every week to satisfy this need. The oxtail also helps Mike maintain jaw strength and provides environmental enrichment for him.

*Wendy Day*

### Does Mike get cold in the winter or hot in the summer?

Wild tigers live in areas with climates much like the climate in Baton Rouge. It gets very hot in the summer in the areas where tigers are found in the wild. Some wild tigers live in areas where it also gets very cold in the winter. While it doesn't get quite that cold in Louisiana, as the weather cools in Baton Rouge in the fall, Mike's coat gets thicker. This keeps him warm in the winter. He sheds his extra hair in the spring as the weather warms. In the heat of the summer, Mike stays cool by lying in the shade and by getting into his pool.

Christine Russell

### Why does Mike pant so much?

Like other cats, tigers only sweat through the pads of their feet. So they cannot rely on sweating to keep them cool. Tigers are able to dissipate some heat by panting. But just because a tiger is panting doesn't necessarily mean that it's too hot. Tigers also pant when they are excited. For this reason, Mike will often pant when he goes to football games even when the outside temperature is mild.

Tim Morgan

### Is Mike's tongue rough like that of a house cat?

Yes, his tongue feels very much like that of a house cat, only much larger!

### Why does Mike sleep so much?

Cats, including tigers, naturally sleep up to about 16 hours per day. Also, because they are nocturnal animals, tigers often sleep during the heat of the day and are more active in the cool of the night.

*Christine Russell*

*Christine Russell*

### Why does Mike walk around his yard so much?

Wild tigers are known to travel up to forty miles per day patrolling their home range. This is especially true for male tigers. They want to make sure that there are no other male tigers in their area. And, they want to know if there are female tigers around. So, even though he is in a much smaller area than a wild tiger, this behavior is completely normal for Mike.

### Why is Mike kept inside at night?

Animals need a period of total darkness each day for good health. Because of the outdoor lights on campus, Mike needs to be kept in his house at night to benefit from complete darkness.

*Ginger Guttner*

*Adam Caro*

bothered by crowds. A few things do seem to bother him a bit. For example, he doesn't like some of the loud music played in front of the PMAC on football game days. He also doesn't like the fireworks that are occasionally used in Tiger Stadium before the games. But his agitation is temporary and seems to disappear quickly. Most of the time that Mike is in Tiger Stadium he is very calm, at times almost going to sleep.

### Is Mike bothered by having so many people around him or by anything else?

Mike is a calm and confident tiger who seems to enjoy being around people. So he is not

### Does Mike play? Does he get bored?

Mike's habitat was designed to include a variety of views and things to do. In addition, Mike seems to enjoy watching people as they pass or move about in front of the enclosure. Also, Mike's caretakers give him toys and place various interesting scents around his habitat. Finally, Mike interacts daily with his caretakers and likewise responds to people who visit him on a regular basis and whom he has come to recognize. All these factors work together to enrich his environment and minimize boredom. It is not like being in the wild—but then Mike also does not have to deal with all of the challenges of the wild, such as diseases, shortage of food, having to kill his prey, and having to compete with other tigers for food and space. Mike's general health and behavior suggest that his habitat is sufficiently interesting and that he is not bored.

Mike's boomer ball does not last long because of punctures by his teeth.

*Bobbie Grand*

### Does Mike recognize his caretakers? If so, how?

Mike certainly does recognize his caretakers. He identifies them by sight, voice, and by the way each of them imitates his "chuff" sound. Both Mike I and Mike V knew the sound of their caretaker's car door closing. Mike VI knew one of his caretakers by the scent of her perfume.

### Does Mike get lonely?

Tigers are naturally solitary animals, and simply keeping them in captivity will not change those instincts. It is not normal for adult tigers to live together, though if they know each other from their youth they can adapt to such a living arrangement. Tigers are solitary animals largely because of the way they capture their prey. Unlike lions, who hunt together, tigers are "ambush hunters." They do not chase their prey in the jungle. Instead, they pounce. So, they naturally do not want other tigers around who might scare off their prey. In the wild, tigers get together only to breed and then separate again. The ranges of a few female tigers will overlap the range of a male, while the ranges of the males do not overlap. It can be very dangerous to introduce one adult tiger to another. There would certainly be a terrible fight, and if one were a female, she would probably be killed.

Mike IV demonstrates the flehmen response, which is the ability to detect scent at the molecular level using a special organ near the nasal cavity.

*Jim Zietz, University Relations*

Caretaker Nick has a tête-à-tête with Mike.

*Christine Russell*

**Have any of the Mikes been female?**

No. By tradition, all of the Mikes have been males.

**Why doesn't LSU breed its tigers so that one is always available?**

There are many reasons for LSU not to establish a tiger breeding program. First, because tigers are solitary animals, they do not normally live together. Putting two tigers together to breed is risky. It is very likely that they will fight and become injured, perhaps even to the point of death. When Mike I was taken to the R. M. Taylor Zoo in Jackson, Mississippi, in 1945 to be mated to a female tiger, he had to return to LSU still a bachelor. After Mike and his intended mate had had several months of fence line contact, officials felt that the tigers still appeared too aggressive toward one another to risk putting them together.

Also, having more than one tiger increases risk and liability for the university. In addition, providing the proper care for tigers is expensive. Supporting multiple tigers is not the best use of limited state or institutional resources. There is currently a surplus of tigers available in captivity. It makes more sense to provide a home for a tiger that really needs one, such as the cub that became Mike VI, rather than contribute to the overpopulation of captive tigers. Finally, there is no way to accurately predict how long each Mike will live and so no way to predict when the next Mike will be needed.

**Have all of the Mikes been related to one another?**

As far as we know, none of the tigers have been related. Other than the second Mike II and Mike III likely coming from the same zoo, they have all come from different sources without any indication that they were related.

**Is there only one Mike, or does LSU have another tiger that just goes to the football games?**

Other than a short period when the adult Mike IV and the cub Mike V were on campus at the same time, there has always been only one Mike the Tiger at a time. Mikes IV and V were on campus together because Mike IV had not yet retired to the Baton Rouge Zoo.

**Why does Mike miss some of the football games?**

Occasionally Mike will not load into his trailer on game day. Sometimes his caretakers can identify the reason, and sometimes they cannot. He seems to not like the loud music played in front of the PMAC on game day, and so when that is playing he may not load. On those days he just prefers to stay in his night house. When Mike goes to football games, it is because he has chosen to load into his trailer.

*Mike looks so calm in Tiger Stadium. Is he ever given sedatives or other drugs to get him to load into his trailer or to keep him calm on football game days?*

No. Mike loads voluntarily into his trailer. If sedation were necessary to load him, then we would not take him to the games. Likewise, Mike is never sedated or given any other drugs to help him remain calm in Tiger Stadium. Each tiger that serves as Mike is carefully selected for qualities and characteristics compatible with the needs of LSU. Dr. Baker selected Mike VI in part because of his calm, confident, and interactive nature. Because he is this way, he remains quite calm even while in Tiger Stadium.

Nicholas Cross and Randee Monceaux with Mike VI at an LSU-Georgia game in 2012.
*Christine Russell*

At the CASA annual fundraiser.
*Christine Russell*

*Why doesn't anyone ever walk Mike around in Tiger Stadium on a leash?*

Mike is not a pet. He is not a trained animal or a circus animal. He is a wild animal living in captivity. While he is relatively tame, that does not mean that he is safe. It is essential that much caution be used when working with Mike.

*Why doesn't Mike go to Mardi Gras parades and fundraisers as he did in past decades?*

Taking Mike out on the highway in his trailer entails a certain amount of risk. In fact, over the history of the tiger mascot program, Mike I was involved in two traffic accidents and Mike III in one accident. There is even more traffic on the roads now than there was back in those times. For that reason, Mike's trips off campus are kept to a minimum. Each summer

Mike attends a fundraiser for the Capital Area Court Appointed Special Advocate (CASA) Association in Baton Rouge, a nonprofit organization of volunteers who serve as advocates for children moving through the court system on their way to foster care or adoption.

### Does Mike attend other LSU sports events besides football games?

Every other year, Mike attends a home baseball game so that the Athletic Department can honor the veterinary student caretakers who have cared for him for the previous two years. This occurs a few days before they graduate from veterinary school. Mike rarely attends other athletic events. Mike the Tiger represents all LSU student athletes, but his closest and longest association is with the football program.

### Does LSU participate in the Tiger Species Survival Plan set up by the Association of Zoos and Aquariums?

As Mike V aged, LSU looked into becoming a site for the Tiger SSP. In the end, the university administration concluded that the restrictions and requirements that would be placed on the university were not acceptable. These included the restriction that Mike could not travel into Tiger Stadium before football games. Also, if Mike was needed to breed a female tiger at another Tiger SSP site elsewhere in the country,

LSU would have to send him to the other site, where he would remain for up to several months.

## TIGER TRADITIONS

- When LSU was a military school, cadets were required to salute Mike and say, "Good morning, Mike."

- The tradition used to be that the football team would score one touchdown for every time Mike roared before the game. Many years ago, Mike was prodded with a broom handle to get him to roar. Now it is no longer allowed to provoke Mike to roar.

- Mike is pulled around the stadium before each game, with the cheerleaders riding atop his trailer leading cheers.

- Mike's trailer is parked next to the opposing team's locker room. When they take the field, they must run past Mike.

- Until the 1970s, Mike's trailer was kept covered as he was brought into the football stadium. It was uncovered, and Mike revealed, only just before kickoff. This was done to build suspense for the game and for Mike's appearance.

- Mike is the only live tiger mascot residing on a university campus.

Mike receives visitors at his former cage. The habitat of the LSU mascot has long been a favorite rendezvous on campus.

*Jim Zietz, University Relations*

- Because cats are more active at night, the story goes that the football team will play better when games are scheduled at night.

- "Meet me at Mike the Tiger's cage."

## TIGER SONGS AND POEMS

### Hey, Fightin' Tigers

Hey, Fightin' Tigers, fight all the way.
Play, Fightin' Tigers, win the game today.
You've got the knowhow, you're doing fine.
Hang on to the ball as you hit the wall,
And smash right through the line.
You've got to go for a touchdown,
Run up the score.
Make Mike the Tiger stand right up and roar.
　　ROAR!!!
Give it all of your might as you fight tonight,
And keep the goal in view: Victory for L-S-U!

### Tiger Rag

Long ago, way down in the jungle
Someone got an inspiration for a tune,
And that jingle brought from the jungle
Became famous mighty soon.
Thrills and chills it sends through you!
Hot! So hot, it burns you too!
Though it's just the growl of the tiger,
It was written in a syncopated way.
More and more they howl for the Tiger,
Everywhere you go today:
They're shoutin':
Where's that Tiger! Where's that Tiger!
Where's that Tiger! Where's that Tiger!
Hold that Tiger! Hold that Tiger!
Hold that Tiger!

## The Coming of Tiger Mike

BY MARVIN N. LYMBERIS

Come, ye children, lean this way,
And learn of the far-famed "Tiger Day."
'Twas back in the year of 'thirty-six—
    Ah, well I do remember
That the Ole War Skule made history
    On the twenty-first day of November.
The sun had not yet pierced the sky,
    When from the dead of night
The entire corps, two thousand strong,
    Made plans to greet "Tiger Mike."
A council of war was hastily called,
    And quickly did they reach
The conclusion that there could be no school
    Without any profs to teach.
So at every gate, a company formed,
    Resolved that no car should pass.
Banners were made and songs were sung,
    "No books, no profs, no class."
And when at last the mighty cat
    Did show itself on site,
The crowd went wild and cheered aloud
    For mascot "Tiger Mike."
No man or beast has e'er before
    Been greeted with such ovation—
Students, prexy, and commandment
    Joined hands in celebration.
For presidents and such may come and go,
    And their memory may die overnight,
But through the years, no one can forget
    The coming of "Tiger Mike."

## The Bengal Bye

A POEM WRITTEN IN HONOR OF MIKE I
BY MR. O. C. HUPPERICK (THE "BENGAL BARD")

I recollect the day when you became
    A growing mascot of our LSU
And how you were displayed at every game
    In festive pride and with affection too.
You had a home on wheels and in a cage
    Where people visited your college sphere
Until you reached the climax of your age
    Which marked the end of your brief visit here.
The Reaper favors no beast or man
    And so your cage becomes an empty cell;
But, "Mike," you had another home as well
    Within the heart of every loyal fan . . .
And each new team shall help exemplify
    A tiger spirit that shall never die.

# All about Tigers

People are naturally curious about tigers. Their beauty and power have intrigued mankind throughout history. The tiger has a major place in some of the world's great religions, and it is not by accident that the tiger is the most written about animal in Asia. In fact, of all animals represented in art around the world and throughout human history, it is claimed that the tiger has been featured more often than any other animal.

Many ask, "What are the advantages of keeping a Bengal tiger mascot?" This is a very good question. Some might quickly respond that maintaining the great LSU Tiger tradition is reason enough. To many, Mike the Tiger is a unique and rousing symbol of the university and represents all that is good about LSU. But Mike is more than a symbol of a great school. He represents all tigers of the world. Indeed, he represents all the endangered animals with which we share this planet. In this respect, Mike provides an excellent and unparalleled opportunity to teach students, staff, faculty, and visitors about the plight of the world's endangered animals. Education is the primary function of the university. It is fitting that LSU use every opportunity, including our beloved mascot, to educate and thereby serve as a positive force in our community and the world.

## TIGER SUBSPECIES

Conservationists currently recognize six extant subspecies of tigers based on geographical location and differences in appearance.

Physical features used to characterize subspecies include size, color, number and pattern of stripes, and skull size. However, scientists have begun conducting molecular DNA studies to determine the true relatedness of different populations of tigers. Genetic analyses suggest that there are no true subspecies and that tigers only appear different because of adaptations to local environments. This view may eventually result in a shift away from efforts to preserve subspecies and toward a greater focus on maintaining the great variation within the tiger population. For now, we will retain the historical view, and will assume that there are six living subspecies. The living tigers include:

Bengal (*Panthera tigris tigris*). Also known as the Royal Bengal or Indian tiger, this is the least endangered subspecies of tigers. This subspecies includes tigers with white or, less commonly, black or golden tabby ("strawberry") color mutations. Male Bengal tigers weigh between about 390 and 570 pounds. The current natural range of the Bengal tiger includes areas of India, Nepal, Bangladesh, Bhutan, and northwest Myanmar. There are approximately 2,500 wild adult Bengal tigers. Most of them live in protected areas.

Indochinese (*Panthera tigris corbetti*). The natural range of this subspecies, also known as Corbett's tiger, comprises most of the jungles

The Bengal tiger (*Panthera tigris tigris*) is the least endangered subspecies of tiger.

*wildxplorer*

of southern Asia, including southern China, Myanmar, Thailand, Vietnam, Laos, Cambodia, and Malaysia. Indochinese tigers are smaller than the Bengal tiger, with males usually weighing between 330 and 420 pounds. It is estimated that only about 350 wild Indochinese tigers live within their natural range.

Malayan (*Panthera tigris jacksoni*). The Malayan tiger was only designated a subspecies in 2004. The Malayan tiger is confined to the southernmost part of the Malay Peninsula. With males weighing about 260 pounds, the Malayan tiger is the smallest of the mainland tiger subspecies. It is estimated that only about 500 Malayan tigers remain.

Siberian (*Panthera tigris altaica*). Also called the Amur, Manchurian, or Northeast China tiger, the Siberian is the largest tiger. Male Siberian tigers normally average about 500 pounds, but some can grow much larger. The heaviest Siberian tiger reportedly weighed in at over a thousand pounds! This subspecies' current range is wooded areas of far eastern Siberia. The estimated wild population is less than 400.

South China (*Panthera tigris amoyensis*). Also known as the Chinese, Amoy, or Xiamen tiger, the South China tiger has the fewest stripes and is relatively small. The males weigh only about 280 to 390 pounds. The current range of South China tigers is limited to wooded areas of eastern China. They are

The Indochinese tiger (*Panthera tigris corbetti*) is smaller than the Bengal.
*Barbara Von Hoffmann/Animals, Animals*

The largest tiger is the Siberian (*Panthera tigris altaica*).
*Mark Stouffer/Animals, Animals*

The South China tiger (*Panthera tigris amoyensis*) has the fewest stripes and the smallest population in the wild.

*Save China Tigers*

spread out over more than twenty tiger reserves, making it difficult for them to find one another. As a result, the South China tiger is the most critically endangered subspecies of tiger, and among the ten most endangered animal species on the planet. In fact, there is concern that this tiger may already be extinct in the wild since a recent survey found none, leaving only a few dozen captive South China tigers to continue the subspecies. It is hoped however, that reintroduction ("rewilding") programs may reestablish the South China tiger in the wild.

Sumatran (*Panthera tigris sumatrae*). With

The Sumatran (*Panthera tigris sumatrae*) is the smallest of the living tigers.

*C. C. Lockwood*

males weighing only 220 to 310 pounds, the Sumatran tiger is the smallest of living tigers. The Sumatran tiger also has the most pronounced "ruff," or collar of hair around the head. This tiger inhabits the jungles of Indonesia (Sumatra). It is estimated that only about 400 to 500 Sumatran tigers live in the wild, making it one of the most critically endangered tigers. There is evidence suggesting that fragmentation of Sumatran tiger populations may be leading to the development of a separate subspecies.

Apart from the living subspecies, three subspecies of tigers have become extinct. (Despite its popular name, the long-extinct sabertooth tiger was not really a tiger.) The following subspecies are extinct:

Balinese (*Panthera tigris balica*). The Balinese or Bali tiger was the smallest of the tigers, weighing only about 200 pounds. This tiger occupied the Bali islands of Indonesia. It was declared extinct in 1970 but had not been seen since 1937.

Javan (*Panthera tigris sondaica*). The Javan tiger occupied the islands of Javan Indonesia. It was about the size of the Sumatran tiger. The Javan tiger was declared extinct in 1972.

Caspian (*Panthera tigris virgata*). Also known as the Hyrcanian or Turan tiger, the Caspian was a relatively large tiger, with males weighing about 530 pounds. The Caspian tiger roamed the sparsely wooded areas of northern

The Malayan tiger (*Panthera tigris jacksoni*) was designated a subspecies in 2004.
*tiger-pictures.net*

Afghanistan, northern Iran, eastern Turkey, western Mongolia, and southern Russia. It was declared extinct in 1980 but had not been seen for many years before that. Its closest living relative is the Siberian tiger, with whom it shares considerable genetic similarity.

## TIGER HABITATS

Tigers live in wooded areas that range from tall grasslands with few trees to thick forests to nearly impenetrable jungles. The amount of territory claimed by a male tiger is determined primarily by two things: the quantity of food and, less importantly, the presence of female tigers. In India, where prey is abundant, a male's territory may be as small as eight square miles. At the other extreme, in Siberia, where prey is scarce, a male tiger may require over one hundred square miles. Typically a tiger's territory is about twenty to thirty square miles. Other environmental factors, such as the presence of water, also affect territory size. Tigers are excellent swimmers, easily crossing bodies of water up to five miles across.

## TIGER SOCIAL LIFE

Because of their method of hunting and capturing prey, wild tigers live alone for most of their adult lives. Tigers stalk their prey, often through dense forest or brush. A tiger will approach to within fifty to one hundred feet of its target before making a short charge, usually from behind. So for tigers, two's a crowd. Another tiger might frighten off the prey, and both would go hungry. Even alone, tigers fail to capture their prey more often than they succeed.

## TIGER REPRODUCTION

If tigers are solitary animals, how do we get more tigers? While tigers live alone most of the time, they do get together for breeding. In fact, the territories of two or more females are often within the territory of a male, though they rarely encounter one another. The territories of two males, however, never overlap. Although tigers are solitary, they form a complex society. They leave scent markings with urine and feces and with glands on their paws. They also put scratches on trees and roll on the ground to let other tigers know of their presence. In these ways tigers remind one another of their territorial boundaries. Even Mike leaves these markings, though he lives alone. Many unsuspecting visitors, standing a little too close to his fence, have been marked as Mike's "territory"! When the female tiger is ready to mate, she will seek out and become very friendly toward the male. Tigers may breed hundreds of times over the course of about a week—about every fifteen minutes when the female is at her peak of receptivity.

The gestation period is about 102 days. Cubs weigh about two pounds when born. While up to five cubs may be born in one litter, two or three is the more common number. Females typically produce a litter every two to three years. Cubs are entirely dependent on their mother for the first six months of life. Then she begins to teach them to hunt for themselves. By about eighteen months, they can go off on their own and fend for themselves. The young females tend to remain with their mothers longer than the young males. Both sexes reach reproductive maturity at around three years of age. Of every one hundred tigers born, only about twenty will survive to reproduce.

When fully grown, male tigers usually

weigh about four to five hundred pounds, depending on their subspecies. Female tigers generally weigh about one hundred pounds less than their male counterparts. The natural life span of a wild tiger is eight to twelve years, with a maximum of about fifteen years. Diseases, injuries, poaching, and starvation exact a heavy toll, especially on males. In captivity, tigers do not encounter these threats, so they generally live longer. Most tigers in captivity live fourteen to eighteen years. Except for Mike II, the LSU tigers have enjoyed remarkably long and healthy lives. Three of the LSU tigers lived over nineteen years.

## TIGER DIETS

Tigers will eat almost anything that moves. Their favorite foods are deer and wild pigs, though they can kill animals as large as water buffalo. In fact, tigers are the only predators of large hoofed animals in Asia. These animals are so important to the survival of the tiger that where they have disappeared, the tiger has soon followed. Tigers eat ten to fifteen pounds of food at a time, staying with the kill until they have eaten it all. A male will make about fifty major kills per year, and a breeding female will make up to around seventy. Tigers eat nearly the whole carcass, not just the muscle meat. In this way they obtain all the nutrients they need.

## IDENTIFYING TIGERS

At first glance, all tigers may appear to look alike. However, tigers can be identified by their stripe patterns. No two tigers have exactly the same striping, just as no two humans have the same fingerprints. Nobody knows why tigers have stripes. It is probably to conceal them from their prey. The Sumatran tiger has the most stripes, and the South China tiger has the fewest. It is a common misconception that tigers can be reliably identified by their footprints, or pug marks. In fact, pug marks change over time. As a tiger gains or loses weight, grows, experiences injuries to the foot pads, and ages, the marks change.

## CAPTIVE TIGERS

While there has been a terrible loss of tigers from the wild, there is no shortage of tigers in captivity. It is estimated that there may be up to fifteen thousand captive tigers in the United States alone, more than twice the number of wild tigers in the world. But if there are so many tigers in captivity, why does LSU need one? First, the vast majority of captive tigers are privately owned and not available for viewing by the public. Consequently they provide no opportunity for educating the public. An important reason for having Mike is the educational benefit that comes from having over 100,000 people per year visit him. He is an

# TIGER HABITATS

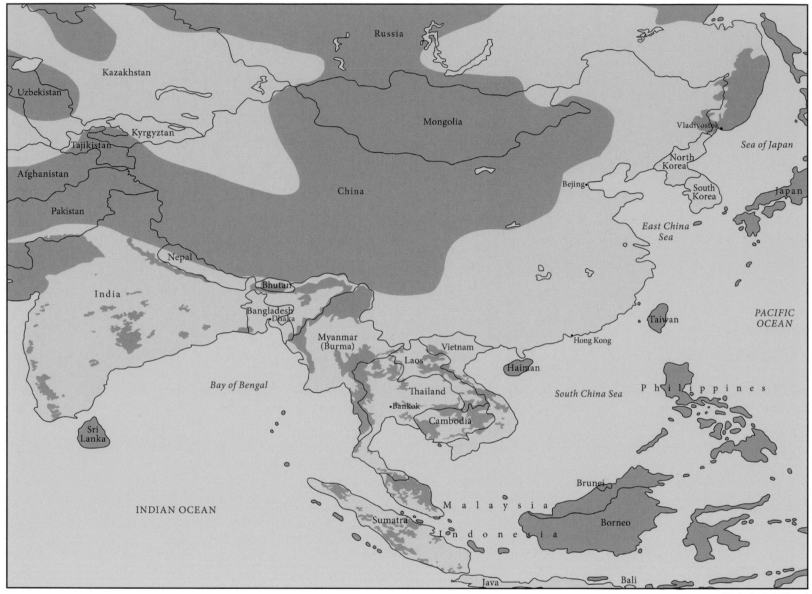

Map by Emily S. Manuel

HISTORICAL RANGES

CURRENT RANGES

142

individual tiger, but he also represents all tigers, as well as all endangered animals. Second, many of the tigers in the United States are owned illegally. An alarming number of "sportsmen" are willing to pay two thousand to twenty thousand dollars to "hunt" a tiger. This often involves shooting a tiger in a fenced area or even in a cage. This gruesome practice is surprisingly common. It is estimated that there may be more than a thousand "canned hunt" providers in the United States. It is hoped that those who visit Mike will gain a greater appreciation of tigers and will help to combat the inhumane killing of tigers in such "hunts."

## TIGER CONSERVATION

As recently as 1900, up to 100,000 tigers roamed the woods and jungles of Asia. Subspecies of tigers lived as far west as Turkey and the Caspian Sea. They ranged as far north as southeastern Russia and as far south as the islands of Indonesia. Today, it is thought that between three and four thousand tigers remain in the wild. However, the tiger is a very difficult animal to count, and it is feared that the actual number may be lower. The remaining wild tigers are scattered among about 160 isolated populations, or tiger conservation units. Loss of habitat, inadequate food sources, poaching, and population fragmentation have decimated wild tiger populations. The natural range of tigers has declined as huge tracts of forest have been cleared for timber or farming. Only relatively small patches of forest remain. With the loss of habitat and the hunting of wild game for human consumption, once abundant prey has also become much harder to find. Loss of prey is the single most important factor in the reduction in tiger populations. Lack of natural prey causes tigers to kill livestock and occasionally humans, resulting in the killing of tigers by local villagers. In addition to these challenges, tigers are poached for their body parts, which are superstitiously believed to have medicinal value. For example, the eyeballs are thought to cure epilepsy; the whiskers, toothaches; the brain, laziness and pimples; the tail, skin diseases; and the bones are believed to cure rheumatism, weakness, and paralysis. Lastly, fragmentation of habitat likewise separates and fragments tiger populations. The remaining tigers are so spread out that they cannot find one another for breeding or they repeatedly breed within a small group, resulting in a weakened gene pool.

There is no doubt that like many other animal species, the tiger is in grave danger of extinction in the wild. Yet there are some exciting and encouraging efforts under way to save the tiger in its natural habitat and to establish genetically healthy captive breeding populations of each of the six tiger subspecies. One of the most important advances in tiger conservation was the creation of a species survival plan (SSP). An SSP is a cooperative management program administered by the American Zoo and Aquarium Association (AZA) with input from scholarly conservation organizations. A number of SSPs have been developed to conserve wild populations of endangered species, including the tiger. The programs seek to establish and oversee healthy captive stocks of endangered animals, mostly in the United States. These animals serve as reservoirs of genetic material that, under tightly controlled guidelines, can be used to reestablish or revitalize wild populations.

Once an SSP has been created, selected American zoos holding the particular animal species work together to form a master plan for managing the species. The master plan includes recommendations concerning mate selection, shipment of individual animals for breeding purposes, and support for other programs designed to protect the species in the wild. The tiger SSP was the first SSP adopted by the AZA. In 1988, the tiger SSP master plan made recommendations concerning the numbers of each of the tiger subspecies that should be held in captivity. In 1992, the plan was modified to include about a hundred tigers from each subspecies. These tigers are to be housed in participating zoos across North America. The plan also called for cooperation with other regional programs, such as those in Europe, India, and Southeast Asia.

In addition to the AZA's tiger SSP, international efforts are under way to save the tiger. For example, Project Tiger, established in India in 1973, has resulted in the creation of over twenty-five tiger reserves in reclaimed land where humans are not allowed to live. Early successes with increasing the Bengal tiger population were tempered by an increase in poaching. The government of India responded by relocating villagers to minimize human-tiger encounters, organizing a Tiger Protection Force to control poaching, and forming additional reserves. The government also supports programs to reintroduce captive-bred tigers into established reserves.

Over the past forty years, many national and international laws, guidelines, and regulations have been developed to protect the tiger. The most important international agreement protecting tigers from poaching is the Convention on International Trade in Endangered Species of Wild Fauna and Flora (CITES). The CITES bans international trade in tigers and tiger body parts. Currently, 175 countries are signatories to the CITES agreement, which requires member countries to actively enforce efforts to prevent illegal trade practices. Unfortunately, enforcement of CITES policies is spotty, with several signatory countries not doing all that they should to protect tigers and prohibit trade in tiger parts. Violations of CITES policies have occasionally resulted in application of trade sanctions against wayward countries. These punitive steps have generally improved compliance.

Regional conservation efforts have also been organized in range countries, where tigers are found in the wild. The Global Tiger Forum is a regional agreement initiated in India in 1994. The forum includes representatives of several range countries and seeks to eliminate trade in tiger parts, support tiger habitats, and promote training and research in tiger conservation. Support for these programs has also come from nonrange countries. In 1999, the United Kingdom became the first—and to this day remains the only—non-tiger-range country to join the Global Tiger Forum. Several local governments in Asia have also enacted laws to protect the tiger. Enforcement of these laws has been inconsistent.

In the United States, there are several federal laws and regulations that prescribe the conditions under which tigers may be kept and that prohibit trading in tigers and tiger parts. Among them, the Animal Welfare Act, administered by the United States Department of Agriculture (USDA), stipulates the housing, transportation, and medical requirements of institutional or private ownership of tigers, as well as many other species of exotic animals.

USDA veterinarians regularly inspect facilities housing tigers and evaluate the standard operating procedures used to care for them. In addition to these federal efforts, most states have enacted laws regulating or banning trade in tigers. More importantly, many states have enacted laws that specifically target canned tiger hunts.

Tiger conservation is at a crossroads. The fate of the tiger will be determined within the next generation. For the tiger to be saved, more cooperation is needed between national and international governing bodies. These groups must no longer initiate "top-down" programs that fail to address the very real problems faced by villagers who frequently suffer loss of property or life from wild tigers. Likewise, local governments must address the quality-of-life issues of those who need and rely on the natural resources found in the tigers' territories. And finally, governments must address the health needs of their people so that the demand for tiger parts for use in traditional Chinese medicine can be eliminated. Effective and culturally acceptable medical substitutes for tiger parts, particularly bone, must be found. These might include parts harvested from cows, pigs, and other agricultural animals. Fundamental changes are also needed in the interactions between groups that work with captive and those that work with wild tigers. Those concerned with saving the tiger in the wild and those whose primary emphasis is on captive tigers must grasp more fully that they are working toward a common goal. Zoos are no longer simply entertainment centers but have become integral players in tiger conservation. To some degree, LSU also has a role to play in this effort, as the university seeks to educate our community concerning conservation issues. The great LSU tradition of Mike the Tiger has itself evolved from one of simply enhancing school spirit to participation in the noble and global effort to save one of the earth's most magnificent animals.

# Acknowledgments

Anyone who has been involved in the care of Mike the Tiger over the years knows that it is far more than any one person can do. While the veterinarians are frequently in the limelight, many people behind the scenes deserve heartfelt thanks for the parts they have played in caring for our precious mascots. The student caretakers, most of whom are now doctors of veterinary medicine or other successful professionals, have provided over seventy-five years of outstanding day-to-day care for the tigers. One of our greatest joys has been to observe the change in our student caretakers as the responsibility of caring for Mike molds them into mature, dedicated professionals.

Our wives and children also deserve recognition for allowing us time away from home during the many hours we have spent caring for Mike, taking him to various events, and telling his story to audiences of all kinds. Our care of Mike has largely been provided after normal working hours, on our personal time. In addition, as we have each served as Mike's veterinarian, we have been on call twenty-four hours a day, seven days a week. This is a sacrifice for any family.

The university and local communities have provided much-needed support for our tigers. From the beginning, the Athletic Department has graciously provided most or all of the financial resources for Mike's care. In addition, several Athletic Department employees past and present have done their part to keep

Mike's enclosures in working order. The LSU Police Department provides security for Mike both on and off campus while the LSU grounds crew works tirelessly to keep Mike's yard beautiful in spite of his playful but destructive habits. Doug Guidroz and Rick Vallet of Central Hitch and Equipment generously provided Mike's current traveling trailer, while Troy LeBlanc, Randy Owens, and other good people at All Star Automotive repainted the trailer free of charge, in the hopes that it will last as long as the previous trailer.

Without the resources of the Veterinary School, it would not be possible to give such special animals the kind of care they deserve. Dr. Rhett Stout has quietly provided over sixteen years of backup coverage, without compensation, for Mike's medical care, since federal law requires that a veterinarian be available to care for the tiger's medical needs at all times. Several other excellent clinicians in the LSU School of Veterinary Medicine have also freely given of their knowledge, skills, and expertise to assist with Mike's care.

Likewise, Dr. Gordon Pirie of the Baton Rouge Zoo has been our friend, adviser, and a faithful assisting veterinarian for Mikes IV, V, and VI. The willing staff of the Baton Rouge Zoo, under the leadership of former director George Felton and current director Phil Frost, took Mike IV and Mike V in as guests when additional housing was needed. They cared for Mike as if he were one of their own. Bob Cooper and the staff of the Little Rock Zoo generously accommodated Mike IV in 1981 while his cage was renovated.

Many people helped make the two editions of this book possible. For the first edition, DeLaine Emmert supplied the energy and enthusiasm that got the wheels turning. Alison Borchgrevink, our faithful and industrious student worker, spent hours ferreting out obscure facts and photos. General Ron Richard (USMC, retired) and the Tiger Athletic Foundation funded Alison's research, and Faye Phillips of LSU's Hill Memorial Library regularly went the extra mile to provide useful historical information. With the assistance of the LSU Alumni Association and several private individuals, we were able to locate and contact nearly all of the former tiger student caretakers, now LSU alumni. These former tiger keepers were very helpful in correcting much erroneous information published in newspapers over the years, ensuring that the material in this book is historically accurate. We also received tremendous support and assistance from Laura Gleason, Maureen Hewitt, Margaret Lovecraft, Catherine Kadair, George Roupe, and Directors Les Phillabaum and MaryKatherine Callaway of LSU Press. The high quality of both the first and second editions of this book is in large part due to their professionalism.

The painting of *The Spirit of LSU* and the etching of Mike III were provided free of charge for use in this book by Glenn Gore. To obtain prints of Mr. Gore's work, visit www .lsuart.net. The painting of Mike V by George Rodrigue was likewise provided free of charge for use in this book by Jacques Rodrigue. To obtain one of these prints, please visit www .georgerodrigue.com.

Many people have given generously of their photographs and time to make this book a vivid representation of the history of Mike the Tiger. For his photographs of Mike V and his assistance in selecting photos for the first edition of the book, we are indebted to C. C. Lockwood. For more information on Mr. Lockwood's work, please visit www .cclockwood.com. Several historically significant photographs were graciously contributed by Jim Amoss and Nancy Burris of the New Orleans *Times-Picayune* and Doug Manship Jr. and Jill Arnold of the Baton Rouge *Advocate*. In addition, private individuals, including several former LSU student tiger caretakers, their friends, and relatives, came forward with interesting information, anecdotes, and photographs. Some of the photographs in this book were obtained through generous donations from Mike's fans and supporters of LSU. While every effort has been made to acknowledge the donors, the source of some photographs and artifacts could not be ascertained. We are especially appreciative of Dr. Phillip Cancilleri, Harry Cowgill, Ginger Guttner, Mark Rayner, Christine Russell, Dr. Tim Morgan, Prather Warren, Michael Westphal, and Jim Zietz for their time and photographic talents.

The personal contributions of so many individuals who cherish Mike the Tiger have made this book special. We express our sincere thanks and appreciation to each one, named and unnamed. We thank you all.

—*David G. Baker and W. Sheldon Bivin*